T0305917

Routledge Revivals

The Functions of Sterling

Why is sterling under pressure? Why was the devaluation in 1967 followed by stagnation of British economy? What do the 1971 monetary reforms mean for sterling in the 1970s? First published in 1973, *The Functions of Sterling* discusses these vital questions and challenges the received wisdom of those who tells us it is beneficial that our money should be worth less. It also examines critically the internal and external performance of sterling throughout the twentieth century. The book argues that the credit control policy offers a real possibility of improved economic growth and encourage the revaluation of sterling. To a large extent the book is in line with Sir Ralph Hawtrey's reasoning and also integrates monetary economics with "real" problems of comparative costs, innovations, and growth.

This book is an essential read for scholars of British economy, public policy, political economy, and economics in general.

The Functions of Sterling

by F. V. Meyer

Routledge
Taylor & Francis Group

First published in 1973
by Croom Helm.

This edition first published in 2021 by Routledge
2 Park Square, Milton Park, Abingdon, Oxon, OX14 4RN
and by Routledge
605 Third Avenue, New York, NY 10017

Routledge is an imprint of the Taylor & Francis Group, an informa business

© 1973 F. V. Meyer

All rights reserved. No part of this book may be reprinted or reproduced or utilised in
any form or by any electronic, mechanical, or other means, now known or hereafter
invented, including photocopying and recording, or in any information storage or
retrieval system, without permission in writing from the publishers.

Publisher's Note
The publisher has gone to great lengths to ensure the quality of this reprint but points
out that some imperfections in the original copies may be apparent.

Disclaimer
The publisher has made every effort to trace copyright holders and welcomes
correspondence from those they have been unable to contact.

A Library of Congress record exists under LCCN: 73176221

ISBN 13: 978-1-032-10299-3 (hbk)
ISBN 13: 978-1-003-21467-0 (ebk)
ISBN 13: 978-1-032-10300-6 (pbk)

The Functions of Sterling

F. V. MEYER

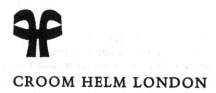

CROOM HELM LONDON

FIRST PUBLISHED 1973
© 1973 BY F. V. MEYER

CROOM HELM LTD 2–10 ST JOHNS ROAD LONDON SWII

ISBN 0–85664–032–8

PRINTED IN GREAT BRITAIN
BY EBENEZER BAYLIS AND SON LTD
THE TRINITY PRESS, WORCESTER, AND LONDON
BOUND BY G. AND J. KITCAT LTD, LONDON

Contents

Contents

Preface

What happens to sterling is not just a matter for finance ministers and central bankers. It affects you and me—and not only in our material rewards but also in the way we work and even how we get on with each other.

A major reform in the management of sterling was introduced in September 1971. It was not the first reform of the management of sterling during the present century and will probably not be the last one. Further changes may come for domestic, European or world reasons, but they will have to develop from the present situation.

The purpose of this book is to explain what happened to sterling in the course of the present century, and so put the 1971 reform into perspective. The book is addressed to the man or woman in Fleet Street, in business and trade unions as well as to the student in the library.

The author wishes to acknowledge his indebtedness to colleagues and students for discussions and comments. Special mention is due to those who have read earlier drafts and helped to improve upon them: Professor L. S. Pressnell, Mr A. R. Culyer, Professor John Black, Mr H. Burton, Mr J. S. Chard, Dr D. C. Corner, Mr M. Macmillen and Mr G. W. P. Wickramasinghe.

Chapter One   THE
FUNCTIONS OF
A CURRENCY

I COMMAND

Sterling, according to the Oxford dictionary, is a genuine coin of standard value. The word can be used to describe anything 'of solid worth' and anything 'that is what it seems to be'. This definition dates from 1911.[1] Linguistically this may still be correct. Economically one may be permitted some doubts, especially since the 1970s started with an unusually sharp rise in prices—and a rise in prices means a corresponding fall in the domestic value of money.

On a year by year comparison, prices rose by 8 per cent in 1970 and 9 per cent in 1971.[2] Although prices had been rising steadily since 1935,[3] such marked increases have few precedents in peacetime in twentieth-century Britain. The first of those precedents occurred in 1920 when prices rose by 14 per cent, but this was associated with an uncontrolled post-war boom. The next occasion was 1948, with 8 per cent, which was a somewhat better controlled post-war boom. The last two precedents were 1950 and 1951, with 9 per cent and 6 per cent respectively. The price movements of those two years are usually attributed to the Korean War boom, though this was probably not the only cause. For instance, the devaluation of sterling in 1949 must have played some part in it. But, whatever may have happened in 1950 and 1951, the early 1970s were the first years of such marked price increases which were not associated with war or post-war problems.

By the time this book is published we will know whether 1970 and 1971 will enter the pages of the history books as

examples of years with exceptional price rises like 1950 and
1951, and whether a period of milder though consistent price
rises will continue. But whatever the future may hold in store,
by 1970 the internal value of the pound was only one-quarter
of what it had been in 1935. Before 1935 it had its ups and
downs but, in so far as it is possible to compare the position
at the beginning of the 1970s with that at the beginning of the
century, the domestic value of the pound had fallen to about
one-eighth of its value in 1900.[4] Around 1900 the pound
sterling was at the height of its value, both at home and
abroad.

The external value of the pound sterling has also been
declining in the course of the present century. Here, too, the
1970s started with an unusual movement. Externally, however,
it was not an unusual fall in value as was the case with the
domestic value of sterling but a rise in exchange value of nearly
7 per cent in the course of 1971.[5] And this movement continued for much of the first half of 1972. In the course of 1970
the external value of sterling had been weakening until
September, as one would expect at a time of unusual inflation.
But inflation was not a British speciality. It was a world-wide
phenomenon. From September 1970 until June 1972 the
exchange rate of sterling rose. At first, this rise was within the
limits of $2·38 to $2·42, the prevailing par value. When
currencies were left to float from August until December 1971,
the rise continued. A new par value of $2·60 was fixed in
December 1971, with permitted variations from $2·54 to
$2·66. The upper limit was not reached but $2·64 was temporarily attained in March 1972, representing a 10½ per cent
rise over September 1970. Otherwise the exchange value varied
between $2·60 and $2·62, from February until May 1972, or
around 9 per cent above the September 1970 rate. In June 1972,
however, confidence broke. Although the higher exchange

value had been maintained without difficulty at a time of continuous balance of payments surpluses and rising exchange reserves and at a time of a slight abatement of the domestic inflation, it came to be believed that the British inflation was continuing at a faster rate than inflation elsewhere. Commentators and markets persuaded themselves that the value of sterling could not be maintained at its present rate for much longer and there was a run on sterling. The authorities decided not to intervene but to let sterling float to find its own value in the market. It floated downwards and seemed to settle around $2·45 until renewed loss of confidence, in October 1972, drove it below the former $2·40 parity.

Thus both the internal and the external value of sterling moved unusually in the early 1970s and they moved in opposite directions, at least for a time. This puzzled many commentators who could not believe that the exchange value of sterling could ever be adjusted in any but a downward direction. For the exchange adjustments of 1931, 1939, 1949 and 1967 were all downwards, and the attempt to restore the pre-1914 parity, in 1925, ended in failure. Opinion was not conditioned to a rise in the exchange rate.

Before 1931, the exchange value of sterling was expressed in gold. It had been fixed at a certain value by Sir Isaac Newton in 1717 and there it remained until 1931.[6] True, this value had to be suspended on occasions as, for instance, during the First World War until 1925. But it was always restored successfully on earlier occasions, and unsuccessfully in 1925. On that last occasion the restoration of the gold standard lasted for only six years. In 1931, it had to be abandoned under the impact of one of the worst economic crises the world had ever seen. The pound was left to depreciate (which means that the authorities let the exchange value fall without fixing a new parity rate). It depreciated by about 30 per cent in terms of gold, though not in terms of other currencies which also lost value. At the time of the outbreak of war in 1939, the pound was devalued by 16 per cent (which means that the authorities fixed a new par value to ensure a low value of sterling relative to the dollar). The pound sterling was devalued again in 1949 by 30·5 per cent and yet again in 1967 by 14·3 per cent. In 1971 the process was reversed by an 8·3 per cent rise in the par value; the first official rise in the exchange rate since 1717. (That sterling rose by slightly less within 1971, and by somewhat more from 1970 to 1972, was due to a corresponding change in the values at which the Bank of England undertook to intervene in the market from a range of $2·38 to $2·42 to one of $2·54 to $2·66 and a rise above $2·60 did not occur until 1972.) But this was a revaluation in terms of dollars without change in the gold parity.

At the time of writing it remains uncertain how the float of mid-1972 will further alter the position. Before the float, the value of sterling in terms of gold was about one-third of what it had been early this century. In terms of dollars the fall in sterling was less, even before the 1971 revaluation, since the dollar too had its difficulties and was left to depreciate and then devalued in the 1930s and again in 1971. In relation to the dollar the fall of sterling was one from a 'traditional' rate of $4·86 to $2·40 before the 1971 revaluation and to $2·60 for a time afterwards—or roughly to one-half of the traditional rate.

From the beginning of this century to the beginning of the 1970s the value of sterling thus halved in terms of dollars, fell to one-third of its former gold parity, and to one-eighth of its former domestic purchasing power. This was not a continuous movement. Sterling rose relative to the dollar at times in the 1930s and again in 1971. Those were times when the authorities did not intervene or did not intervene too much in the exchange markets, and also times when sterling tended to rise relative to the dollar. For the fall in the dollar parity was at least as much the result of deliberate policy as of market forces. The same does not apply to the fall in the gold value and in the internal purchasing power of the currency. The authorities tried to restore its gold value in 1925 but were driven off it in 1931. Changes in the domestic purchasing power of sterling were seldom welcome to the authorities. This applies equally to the fall in prices of the 1920s and early 1930s as to the rising prices during most of the century. Thus the fall in the value of sterling was not continuous and much of it far from deliberate. It was none the less marked. Of course none of the indices of the declining value of sterling is perfect. Changes in the domestic price level are more meaningful from one year to the next than over a long period of time, since the nature of goods and services does not alter too much from year to year but is quite different now from what it was at the beginning of the century. The gold value of a currency is not a perfect index of the value of such currency, unless there is a direct relationship between domestic money supply and the central bank's gold holdings; and while gold mattered at the beginning of the century its chief usefulness now is as one of several ways of holding exchange reserves, and dollars will do just as well. The dollar itself has not been immune from vicissitudes and erosion of purchasing power. Although none of these three indices is perfect, they all point to a secular decline in the value of sterling.

In many ways it does not matter whether the value of a bundle of goods is called £1 or £8. What matters more is whether the price of that bundle of goods rises or falls. Even this does not accurately reflect inflation or deflation, since a rise in prices may reflect improvements in quality and a fall in prices may reflect greater efficiency in production rather than monetary changes. Moreover, even if a rise in prices is due to monetary causes, it is not necessarily harmful. At this point, it may be useful to pause and reflect on what precisely an inflation does. Put briefly, it favours those who earn and spend today over those who earned yesterday and intend to spend tomorrow. Socially, this means inflation raises the economic power of the wage earner and short-term financial operator over that of the old age pensioner and the long-term investor. There is change in economic society but not necessarily growth. The past is at a discount relative to the present, since past savings erode in value. Society becomes less traditional. At the same time the future is at a discount whenever the purchasing power of money is expected to fall, and this discourages long-term planning by potential investors. There is both less tradition and less foresight, and there is more preoccupation with the needs of today. Production becomes more geared to current requirements and investment undertaken for early returns. Long-term savings and investment are discouraged.

From a strictly economic point of view, change is desirable if it allows more goods and services to be created than could otherwise be created. If inflation allows more goods and services to be created for today than are foregone for tomorrow, the change can be commended on economic grounds.[7] As long as the national income rises by more than the rate of inflation, such inflation is not disruptive in an economic sense which is neutral between different organisations of society and different products. It becomes disruptive only if a destruction of past savings exceeds the growth of current output. Thus, between 1900 and 1970, the national income rose about three times as much as prices did,[8] so that over the long period Britain did not suffer from disruptive inflation. Individual years apart, the problem of disruptive inflation did not arise until the post-war period, and not in an acute form until the late 1960s when the rate of inflation accelerated while production decelerated. Even in those years, the inflation can be proved to have been disruptive only if it can be shown that less thought for today would have allowed an appropriate increase in investment.

It will always be a matter of controversy whether inflation in a particular year or years was economically disruptive or just helped to keep economic activity going. Be this as it may for individual years, a prolonged period of disruptive inflation inevitably hampers all long-term tasks. Foremost amongst these is the government of the country which is an unending task. Government is not only a matter of economics. Where there is strong political cohesion, the effectiveness of government may be unimpaired even if there is substantial economic disruption. Nevertheless, even the government itself is not immune from the consequences of what it allows to happen to its money.

The effectiveness of government depends upon how it exercises its power of command. These powers can be divided into physical and monetary ones. The physical power is one of command over men as exercised by the judiciary, the police and the armed forces. The monetary power is a command over resources which does not involve physical force. It is civilian command. These powers of command interact since law and order cost money, while civilian command can be exercised only where there is law and order. Whether a government can be decisive and effective is largely derived from these two powers. For even in its budget the government decides on *how* its powers are to be exercised and not on *what* these powers are. True, in its budget the government tries to predetermine the proportion of monetary command in its own hand and that which is to be left diffused over the private sector; it decides on whom to subsidise and what to tax, and so on. Yet all these budgetary powers are powers over the distribution of monetary command and the budget itself is calculated in terms of money. If the value of money changes, or rather if it changes by more than anticipated at the time the budget was drawn up, the government's budgetary plans go awry. Although a fall in the value of money after budget day does not necessarily frustrate any of the government's decisions on the distribution of monetary command, it means that monetary command itself is less effective. This point has been stressed because in the literature of the last generation much play has been made of budgetary or fiscal policy as an alternative to monetary policy, but fiscal policy is physical power in a monetary garb. If that wears thin all that is left is physical force.

The twentieth-century decline in the value of sterling meant a debasement of sovereignty as exercised through money. As its monetary command became less, the government had to issue more orders just to get the same results. If the origin of the twentieth-century welfare state can be traced to the introduction of social insurance in the 1900s, this did not mean a sudden conversion of the then government to state intervention but was one possible response to a situation when the domestic purchasing power of money was falling.[9] The rise in prices at that time may have been slight by the standards we have since become used to—it was about 1 per cent a year—but meant that the savings of the thrifty could not be so much relied on to save them from calamity. That is only possible if the value of money is stable or rising, at least in relation to food. Protection of key industries and rent control came for strategic and social reasons during the First World War. Had it been possible to restore a stable value of money, rent control at least would have become redundant. When the balance of payments turned adverse in 1931, the experts recommended either the imposition of a general import tariff or the abandonment of the gold standard.[10] Under the pressure of events, the government of the day introduced temporary protection which subsequently became permanent, while the depletion of the Bank of England's gold reserves forced the abandonment of the gold standard. When sterling was subsequently left to depreciate and provided no firm standard of value, protection came to be taken for granted. The subsidisation of depressed industries and areas came to be regarded as a need and detailed regulations of industrial and agricultural activities became acceptable. Central government economic planning and the welfare state were to replace monetary controls in the years of post-war reconstruction of the 1940s. The abandonment of state intervention in the economy did not go as far as some expected to be possible in the 1950s when monetary controls were only imperfectly restored. Difficulties with maintaining the external value of sterling and the domestic price level blew governments of both parties off course in the 1960s. The government elected in mid-1970 sought to stand aloof from the details of economic management but had to retrace its steps less than two years later. Although there had been some tightening of monetary controls in the preceding few years, it had not gone far enough to allow for a dramatic withdrawal of government from the market place. Thus the period from 1900 to 1970 was on the whole one of increasing government control of the economy, and attempted reversals in the early 1970s and on previous occasions never went as far as some might have hoped for. The reason was not so much ideological as that governments had to respond to events. Quite simply, as monetary sovereignty became more and more debased as the century went on, the government had to issue more and more fiscal and physical regulations just to maintain its authority. None of this is an argument either for or against direct government intervention in the details of economic affairs. It is

2

merely asserted that monetary and physical controls are alternative means of command, and when one weakens the other must be strengthened if authority is not to erode.

It is always difficult to know how far monetary controls can be relied on and, by implication, how far non-monetary controls have to be used. Moreover, it is not easy to find the sort of controls, monetary or otherwise, that best fit the age. If no appropriate monetary controls can be found there is no choice—or rather there should be no choice. It has happened, however, for instance in the 1920s, that this was not recognised. Money was exalted too much. Where this is the case, command expressed through money may increasingly become command in a widening void of bankruptcies, unemployment and poverty. The collapse of 1931 still is a warning example of what can happen if the value of money is put too high and economic policy solely directed at maintaining too high a value of the currency. But money can also be ignored too much and its command not heard amongst a clutter of regulations which in turn become increasingly difficult to enforce. This happened in the 1950s and 1960s, when monetary command was weak and the authorities tried to get results through increasingly complex direct regulations of domestic activities. Banks were instructed in what to lend and to whom, builders were told where to build and how, the central government became increasingly concerned with who was to be paid what, and whether consumers should buy what and when and whence.

To do all that effectively would have required more computers than were available just to ensure that each regulation would have the required effect and none counteract any other. It will probably never be known which of the various controls had which effect since they came in 'packages'. All that is clear is that detailed fiscal and physical controls become inescapable when monetary control weakens. At times, there was a case for weaker monetary controls and more protection (which is another way of saying direct controls) as, for instance, in the 1920s and 1930s. The then known monetary controls turned out to be too restrictive when there was mass unemployment at home and world markets were shrinking. Depreciation and protection at least worked in the same direction of providing more employment at home. Given protection, and therefore increased control over external trade, there was at least a possibility of replacing monetary control by domestic regulations which could be isolated from external events.

None of this applied in the 1950s and 1960s. There was no mass unemployment in Britain or elsewhere in the industrial world. Trade barriers fell everywhere. If Britain was to participate in the expansion of world trade she too had to abandon, or at least reduce, external trade controls. It is, however, difficult to participate successfully in international specialisation of a sort which involves long-term investment, if the market is subject to detailed regulations. This is so simply because it is always possible to regulate the known, but extremely difficult to regulate anything which involves a substantial amount of uncertainty. The various regulations normally gave priority to the financing of activities which would show quick and predictable balance of payments results. Effectively this meant priority for known activities. It should thus not be surprising that the economy fell somewhat behind in international competition where much of the rising trade was in previously unknown goods and services. These can be created only after prolonged research and development expenditure and seldom give quick results.[11] Some of these points will be dealt with at greater length below. Here let it suffice to say that increasing freedom in external trade was incompatible with increasing detailed control of internal activities. This problem was not yet resolved by the beginning of the 1970s.

At least some lessons should be learnt from the past. The following two sections set out to show what may be wanted of the monetary system and how its domestic performance affects its external value. The argument will draw freely from the whole of twentieth-century experience of the pound sterling.

2 THE EMPLOYMENT FUNCTION

If it can be said that the value of sterling was sometimes too high and at other times too low, this does not imply that sterling (or any other money) has any value by itself. Its value derives solely from the functions it performs. Now *the function of a currency is to ensure the full and efficient use of resources in its trading area*, where the trading area is anywhere where that currency can be used in settlement of transactions. In relation to this definition, a currency should be regarded as *overvalued* if the economy does not produce enough. It is too difficult to earn that currency to allow for the fullest possible utilisation of employable resources. As will be shown in section 4, the currency should be regarded as *undervalued* if the economy does not produce efficiently enough. Such a currency is relatively easy to earn, with the result that people do not bother to use resources as sparingly and efficiently as their technical skills allow. Both overvaluation and undervaluation, as here defined, can have adverse effects on the external exchange value if people in other economies produce more and better.*

* (It should be noted that not all writers use the terms 'overvaluation' and 'undervaluation' in this way. To some, any currency is overvalued if its dollar exchange rate cannot be maintained for whatever reason, and undervalued if market forces will drive its exchange rate up. This approach is correct if the currency is viewed from outside, but it obscures the causes of the rise or fall of the currency. For instance sterling appears to them as overvalued in the 1920s and again as overvalued in the 1960s. In the 1920s the economy suffered

In this section, the efficiency function of the currency will be largely ignored. The excuse is that it is not possible to write about everything at once. Moreover, at any one point of time production techniques are given. Even within a short period, say from one year to the next, production techniques are still largely given since any change involves rethinking, revised plans, new investment, changed attitudes towards work and uncertainty of how the market will respond. This is one reason why the relevance of the value of the currency to efficiency is none too apparent in the short period and all too easily overlooked. Increasing efficiency implies changes in employment but the twentieth-century problem of the value of sterling first arose in the inter-war years when there was mass unemployment. The major problem was how to make more use of existing resources through an increased volume of employment rather than through greater efficiency per unit produced.

While it is never quite correct to ignore the efficiency function of a currency, for the purpose of exposition it may be convenient to start with the employment function. Part of our definition of the function of a currency was that it should ensure the full use of resources. If efficiency is given, this means full

from mass unemployment but the balance of payments was favourable. In the 1960s, the employment rate was high and the balance of payments was weak. To use the same term for diametrically opposed situations may give the impression that identical remedies are suitable for those diametrically opposed situations. True, the result was the same since in both cases the exchange value of sterling fell. However, if causes as well as results are of interest, identical terminology obscures the issue. It seems preferable to follow Sir Ralph Hawtrey's practice[12] of reserving the term overvaluation to the position in the 1920s, where none seem to quarrel with the view that the currency was then overvalued, and to use the term undervaluation for the position in the 1960s. This defines the value of the currency in relation to the domestic situation. It indicates possible remedies. The meeting ground with those who use 'overvaluation' in relation to the 1960s is that the currency was *misvalued* on both occasions, so that on both occasions the economy was weakened relative to the rest of the world and the currency fell. But it was weakened for different reasons.)

employment without inflation. All employable factors of production are fully utilised and there is no distortion of values through inflation. During the present century such an ideal state of affairs was attained by the United States between 1922 and 1929 but neither before nor since.[13] If Britain ever attained it, it was not in the twentieth century.

Economic activity is not only domestic. A substantial proportion of domestic production is exported, and this adds to employment and the stream of domestic money income. At the same time domestic consumption does not consist of domestic goods alone, but is supplemented by imports; and such imports destroy domestic employment and money incomes. These external transactions too should be in balance. They seldom are, except by accident: Britain attained such external balance in 1933, a year hardly to be commended for its economic performance; and she nearly attained it in 1949 and 1961, which were not outstandingly good years for the British economy.[14]

Since the ideal state of domestic and external equilibrium has so far eluded us, the problem has never been one of how to maintain an equilibrium position but rather how to get away from an intolerable disequilibrium. In all probability, the value of sterling (or of any currency) has never been absolutely right, but its value in relation to the problems of the day could help or hinder the attainment of whatever objectives were desired, such as full employment or growth or external balance.

First consider a situation of persistent and substantial unemployment. The value of the money unit is then too high in relation to the real situation. The money unit is too scarce to allow for the purchase of all the goods that are produced, let alone of all the goods that could be produced. The value of money should be lowered in order to enable the authorities to issue more currency and to allow for an expansion of credit.

If the exchange rate is kept too high, this may not be possible. For the authorities may fear that credit expansion might endanger the convertibility of the currency into gold at a fixed par value or into dollars at a fixed par value. Once this exchange restraint is removed, domestic credit expansion is eased in two ways. One is that the authorities are relieved of their obligation to keep the national money scarce in order to maintain the exchange rate into gold or other currencies, so that they can lower interest rates and remove other credit restraints. The lower cost and greater ease of borrowing staves off some bankruptcies and keeps production going or even expanding. It becomes cheaper to produce.

The other reason is that exporters earn more profits in sterling if sterling is a currency which has fallen in value relative to other currencies. Exporters then receive more sterling for any one dollar (or other foreign currency) earned but the cost of domestic factors of production is not immediately affected. Thus, relative to the profits earned from exporting, the costs of production become less.[15] Exporting becomes more profitable. Production for export becomes relatively cheap.

Thus the point of letting the exchange rate drop is to *produce* cheaply. Since this affects exporters even more than other producers, the hoped-for credit expansion should be export-led, in the sense that exporters benefit first and most. Exporters can make use of their new opportunities either by maintaining the dollar prices of the goods and services and so receive more sterling per unit sold, or they may decide to sell cheap while lowering their dollar prices in the hope of selling larger quantities, or they may choose a position in between those two extremes. In any case, their profits in terms of sterling rise and this should encourage them to expand output. Hence their demand for factors of production should rise and the level of employment should also rise. There is no guarantee that this will happen, but as long as the value of the money unit is kept too high it cannot happen.

An unduly high value of the money unit means that the currency cannot properly fulfil its employment function. Money is hard to get. Not enough men are wanted for economic activities and much existing capital equipment stands idle. An expansion of economic activity then takes primarily the form of re-employment: existing machines are used again and men are taken on the payroll to perform their former tasks once again. They produce again what they produced before. In consequence there are more of the same goods and services and, when the quantity of known goods and services increases, their price per unit tends to fall. By itself such expansion of production would not pay but it can be facilitated if the value of the money unit is lowered sufficiently to make production that much 'cheaper'.

In the home market this does not necessarily pay. Factor prices (such as wages, material costs and interest payments) have fallen *relative* to similar costs in the outside world. If product prices in terms of home currency fall correspondingly, firms are no better off than before and their expansion is frustrated. But if firms do not lower prices by as much as factor costs have fallen, the wage- and salary-earning population have not got the purchasing power to buy what to them are still dear goods and may even be relatively dearer goods. The matter is aggravated where much of the essentials of life, such as food, are imported and imports become dearer in terms of domestic currency as a result of the fall in the exchange rate. In such a case, even less purchasing power may be available for spending on domestically produced goods than before the fall in the exchange rate. Exhortations to firms to sell at lower prices at home and to workers to accept lower wages and salaries then fall on deaf ears, simply because neither side could do so without abandoning at least some of their present spending commitments. Were they to abandon such commitments, the domestic employment situation might be aggravated rather than eased. Hence, if a fall in prices is to be contemplated, it must be a fall in prices charged to foreign consumers in terms of their own currencies which can now be converted into more sterling than before. Such additional sterling receipts can then form the basis of credit expansion.

What matters then is not whether prices to overseas customers are lowered but that receipts in sterling rise. Whether this be achieved through higher sterling prices charged per unit of export or through a larger volume of exports is then a question of secondary importance. In times of widespread unemployment, however, when expansion largely means re-employment and the creation of more known goods, this normally necessitates at least some lowering of prices charged to overseas consumers in order to encourage an expansion of overseas sales.

To sell more at lower prices in terms of foreign currency and yet earn more domestic currency per unit sold sounds deceptively easy and beneficial. It is deceptive for, although any percentage fall in the exchange value of sterling gives individual exporters correspondingly more sterling per unit of foreign currency actually earned, the total amount of foreign exchange receipts of the country does not necessarily rise proportionately. For any 10 per cent fall in the exchange value of sterling (from an index of 100 to one of 90) exports must rise by 11 per cent (from an index of 90 to one of 100) just to give the same overall results in foreign exchange earnings. Unless substantial stocks of goods have accumulated, this is hardly feasible. Generally an appropriate response of exports is more likely when the depreciation or devaluation is slight rather than when it is substantial, since the additional goods and services must be made available for export and markets have to be found for them. If this is not possible in the circumstances prevailing at the time of depreciation or devaluation, there can be no benefit.

Suppose that either domestic or overseas conditions do not allow exports to rise by as much as the exchange rate falls (or imports do not fall as much, or the rise in exports plus the fall in imports does not lead to the same result, so that the growth of *net* exports does not compensate for the fall in the exchange rate). If the currency is still weak—and had it not been weak there would not have been any depreciation or devaluation in the first place—the intended relaxation in credit is impeded. For the exchange reserves are less than they could have been, so that the authorities must be more cautious in relation to domestic credit expansion than they might otherwise have been. If domestic credit is linked to gold, the connection is direct. But even where the link between domestic credit and gold has been severed, as in post-war Britain, the chief reason for domestic credit restraint has almost invariably been fear of loss of exchange reserves. Thus any lowering of the exchange rate can be self-defeating, if it is by a larger percentage than the possible rise of overseas incomes and/or the possible increase of domestic output.

For instance, after 1931 the value of British exports did not re-attain even its depressed 1930 level throughout the decade whether measured in sterling or in dollars; and the balance of payments stayed in deficit. (The balance of payments had been in surplus in the 1920s.)[16] At first sight, the immediate result of the 1949 devaluation looked as if there had been a big Sale on. 1950 saw the biggest balance of payments surplus then on record, only to be followed by an even bigger deficit in 1951. But it was not simply that the country had cleared out its stocks of goods in 1950 and then had not enough goods left for export in 1951. The surplus in 1950 was not only due to devaluation but also to tight import controls at a time when the outside world experienced a boom; while the deficit in 1951 was probably largely the result of the fall in overseas incomes caused by the collapse of the Korean War boom. Subsequently in the 1950s, the position remained precarious and nearly every second year alarm about the state of the exchange reserves led to domestic credit restraint. Quite possibly, the 30 per cent depreciation of 1931 and the devaluation by a similar amount in 1949 were overdoses on balance of payments grounds. The devaluations of 1939 and 1967 were only about half of this amount. Since the 1939 devaluation came at a time of the outbreak of the Second World War, it is impossible to disentangle any consequences it may have had. The 1967 devaluation came in a year when world trade expanded at only about half the rate to which the world had become accustomed at that time.[17] The revival of world trade, in 1968, helped to secure a rise in the dollar value of British exports but the balance of payments did not become favourable until 1969 by which time other measures had intervened.[18] The consequence of the 1967 devaluation will be dealt with at greater length in Chapter 2. Here it is enough to say that the position contrasted sharply with that in 1931 and 1949. There was mass unemployment in 1931, while the fear of a post-war slump and mass unemployment was a major argument in favour of the devaluation in 1949. In 1967 employment considerations played little or no part in the decision to devalue. Nevertheless, as will be shown in Chapter 2, it had its effects on the domestic employment situation but these cannot be commented upon until the efficiency function of the currency has been considered in some detail.

The point which has to be stressed here is that however strong the case for a lowering of the exchange rate may be in particular circumstances, an excessive lowering of that rate may defeat its own ends. Although exporters benefit from the redistribution of sterling income in their favour, if this is accompanied or followed by a further domestic credit restraint, there is no certainty of net benefit to firms which both export and sell at home. Since the majority of firms sell more at home than abroad, even the income and employment effects of devaluation may be frustrated. It may be better to proceed more gradually, as for instance under the International Monetary Fund rules of December 1971. These permit 2¼ per cent variation either side from parity which means a total range of 4½ per cent. This is much more within the realm of what can feasibly be translated into more production and more exports than the more drastic changes attempted through past devaluations, even if it means that the dose may have to be repeated.[19] One or two aspirins a day may cure a headache but thirty taken all at once . . .

None of this denies that on *domestic* grounds a sharp change in the exchange rate may be better than no change in that rate. The abandonment of the gold peg in 1931 may not have helped the balance of payments but it allowed for easier domestic credit. The overvaluation before then had prevented this and depreciation was badly needed in order to facilitate a rise in employment. Although a more gradual change might have been more beneficial even on domestic grounds, this really should have started when unemployment first began to rise ten years earlier. By 1931, a sharp change was better than no change. At least it allowed for recovery from the depths of the slump but it did not go far enough; even in 1937, the best year of the 1930s, there were still nearly 11 per cent of the labour force out of work.[20] What was needed was a continuing further and further relaxation of credit rather than one sharp change with an inadequate follow-up. Again there may have been an argument for a 30 per cent devaluation in 1949, when there was fear of a post-war slump of the 1921 variety and the authorities sought ways of allowing domestic full employment to continue irrespective of what happened in the world outside. If a high level of employment is sought as such, the 1931 depreciation helped too little and the 1949 devaluation helped too much. For after 1931 full employment was not attained and after 1949 there was full employment *with* inflation.

Such domestic consequences are a different matter from any possible balance of payments effects. When there is unemployment at home there is a case for credit expansion in order to make more use of available manpower and equipment. If the exchange rate is too high to allow for this, it is better to let the exchange rate drop in value than to let people drop by the wayside. It is quite another matter to conclude from this that the balance of payments will necessarily improve. For that is limited by the possibilities of realisable domestic growth of output and overseas income.

In the 1930s the chief limiting factor to both domestic recovery and balance of payments recovery was that overseas incomes recovered more slowly than British incomes. In consequence, imports revived more than exports. Had the employment position in Britain improved more than it did, the balance of payments situation might well have been worse. After 1949, it was not possible to produce more of the same goods. The feared post-war slump did not materialise and there were next to no unemployed factors for another twenty years. Although a drastic change may have been better than no change in 1931, and although the 1949 devaluation may have been one of many reasons why there was no 1921 type of post-war slump in 1949 or at any time after the Second World War, in neither case can a beneficial balance of payments effect be demonstrated. In the absence of beneficial balance of payments effects, the result of the drastic fall in the exchange rate was a weakening of sterling. This in turn led to more cautious domestic credit policies than might otherwise have been possible and so frustrated at least some of the domestic prosperity it had been intended to promote.

True, there was some redistribution of income in favour of exporters. This was beneficial to the exporters, though it does not necessarily follow that it was beneficial to exports. It does not even follow that it was, on balance, beneficial to exporting firms. They gained because of the higher sterling receipts from exporting but, since most firms sell more at home than they export, they also lost in so far as excessive depreciation or devaluation led to tighter domestic credit than might otherwise have been necessary. In so far as they benefited, they got more money for selling the same sort of goods abroad. Relatively more money for selling the same goods and services abroad hardly encourages firms to try to sell different goods and services abroad. They were more content as they were.

3 ABSOLUTE ADVANTAGE

It may be said that the argument so far leans rather heavily on the domestic implications of the value of sterling and almost suggests that balance of payments effects were incidental. This may be the lesson of history but in recent years the argument was more usually conducted in terms of the balance of payments, with domestic effects often regarded as incidental. At times of balance of payments weakness the exchange rate is wrong. Confidence in that rate flags and it is likely to fall. If so, it may seem legitimate to conclude without further question that an exchange rate which cannot be maintained must be too high. All other things being equal, it should be lowered voluntarily or it will be forced down. It is then tempting to dub the old rate an 'overvalued' rate which does not allow for enough production for export. If this is legitimate, it is also legitimate to ask why an exchange rate cannot be maintained and whether all other things are really always equal. The answer may well be that the maintenance of the old rate would require policies which are either unknown or unpalatable. Yet it does not seem to be enough merely to recognise that a currency is sick and to prescribe the same remedy for every sickness just because the taste of other medicines is unknown or unpalatable.

In the course of time the term 'overvaluation' came more and more frequently to be applied to the exchange rate of the currency of any country in balance of payments difficulties, no matter what its domestic employment position, its state of development, or its place in the trade of nations. Such countries were deemed not to sell enough because their prices were too high, and this fault was to be remedied by a lowering of the exchange rate. That the basic point of lowering the exchange rate is to produce cheap, rather than to sell cheap, appears to have been increasingly overlooked. To produce cheap is to make more employment practicable but when there is full employment this is impossible. The inherent inconsistency between a devaluation and a fully employed domestic economy is then overcome by alternative ways of making the money unit scarcer, such as credit squeezes and fiscal measures to discourage domestic expenditure. It is curious that such measures should have been taken after the 1967 devaluation in order 'to make devaluation work'[21] when they were taken because devaluation by itself could not, and did not, lead to the hoped-for balance of payments turnround. And at least some of those measures were designed to have the opposite effects on the economy from those a devaluation can have. But this is going too far ahead. The present task is rather to see how 'overvaluation' came to be identified with an unsatisfactory balance of payments performance and devaluation came to be thought of as a suitable remedy for balance of payments difficulties.

The twentieth-century exchange rate problem of sterling first arose in the 1920s, when it became apparent that an economy with an overvalued currency did not make full use of its resources and so did not produce enough for sale anywhere. For, in order to maintain what was then an excessively high exchange value of the currency, credit was kept too tight to allow for full employment. Easier credit could have made production more profitable; and had such additional production paid, more goods and services could have been offered for sale at home or abroad.

Arguments about the exchange rate issue in the 1920s centred around this point and remarkably little attention appears to have been paid to any possible balance of payments implications.[22] The balance of payments was favourable in the 1920s both before and after the restoration of the gold standard in 1925 (except in 1926, the year of the General Strike); and although the first sharp balance of payments deficit of modern times in 1931 caused consternation, the balance of payments was not to hold the centre of economic debate until the 1950s and 1960s. The problem of the 1920s and 1930s was unemployment. The argument was about whether prices could or should be lowered so as to clear the market at then prevailing levels of incomes, or whether money incomes should be raised to match the prevailing levels of prices. Those who favoured low prices sought to achieve this end by forcing the exchange rate up to its pre–1914 parity, and this meant tight credit. They carried the day in 1925 but not for long. The collapse of the exchange rate in 1931 effectively gave the victory of the argument to the incomes school, when at least the worst of the depression was relieved by easier credit—which in turn had been made possible by a lower exchange rate.[23] These arguments are not dead: industrialists and trade unionists are still being exhorted to exercise restraint in pricing (including the pricing of labour) while the authorities' response to mounting unemployment in 1971-2 was a rapid increase in money supply. Had the former exhortations been heeded, the exchange rate might have risen more than it did in 1971-2 and there might have been less of a reaction in mid-1972; while the increase in money supply was effected in deliberate disregard of any possible weakening of the (then rising) exchange rate.[24]

The situation in 1971-2 will be dealt with at greater length in Chapter 2. Here let it suffice to stress again that, in times of persistent unemployment, an unduly high exchange rate acts as a brake on credit and so impedes recovery. The abandonment of the exchange rate restraint can then lead to easier credit and so to re-employment of idle factors of production. The enhanced spending power of the re-employed raises the demand for goods which initially may be met out of stocks. Once stocks are exhausted, employment rises to replenish them. While this is in train, those solely interested in price stability will wish to call a halt to the expansion.[25] Those interested in the attainment of full employment will favour further expansion. Since this implies the creation of money incomes for those engaged in the production of goods which will become available only later on, the rise in money incomes precedes the increase in the quantity of goods available. This may cause a rise in prices which, in turn, raises the profitability of production; but it may also imply some rise in export prices relative to prices prevailing abroad. Devaluation or depreciation forestalls this in so far as it enables a rise in sterling prices to take place without a corresponding increase in prices in foreign currency. The case for helping the export trades through devaluation or depreciation then depends on more goods being in the process of production.

The eventual failure of the attempt to restore the pre-1914 parity in 1925 was a failure to force prices down and so sell cheap and therefore more. The alternative would have been to let the exchange value of sterling depreciate or to devalue it to a lower parity; and this would have made it possible to produce cheap and therefore more. Production would have been more profitable and the price-competitive position in non-sterling markets could have been safeguarded through a lower exchange rate. The policy of 1925 was an attempt to sell cheap. With hindsight, it is possible to say that it would have been better to try to produce cheap so as to raise profits in terms of sterling which in turn would have made it pay to produce more for sale *either at home or abroad*.

Whenever there is widespread and persistent unemployment there is a case for a policy which helps to produce cheap. This was 'the' problem of the 1920s, and not the balance of payments. Some would say the same of the early 1970s. In such circumstances, the chief issue was to raise the *volume* of British economic activity and, externally, the *volume* of British participation in world economic activity. Where this is the chief issue, overvaluation of the currency diminishes the absolute level of activity below the possible level of activity. The removal of overvaluation then can have favourable effects on the country's *absolute* advantage within the world economy. It can have no immediate effects on the country's *comparative* advantage in some activities relative to others. In times of unemployment, when less is produced than could be produced, what matters is to raise the economy's absolute advantage within world economic activity. But when it comes to the question of how to improve a country's balance of payments, what matters is the country's comparative advantage.

Put briefly, the difference is as follows. Devaluation or depreciation can affect the cost price of, say, British beer relative to foreign beer; and it can affect the cost price of, say, British wine relative to foreign wine; and it affects both of those ratios by the same percentage amount. It has no effect on the relative cost price of British beer and British wine, nor has it any effect on the relative cost price of foreign beer and foreign wine. Yet what matters for trading performance is that different amounts of beer and wine can be produced in Britain and abroad. The law of comparative costs tells us that if with a given factor input, Britain can produce relatively more beer than wine compared with the rest of the world, Britain should specialise on beer and the rest of the world on wine. The more commodities become like 'beer' the better will be Britain's trading performance; but this depends upon changes in relative costs of production in Britain compared with the relative costs of production of the same commodities in the rest of the world. These ratios remain unaffected by devaluation or depreciation of sterling or of any other currency. Devaluation or depreciation of sterling can raise the *volume* of activity in Britain compared with the volume of activity in the rest of the world, as long as there are unemployed factors of production in Britain which could be taken into employment. But it does not improve the *kind* of activity which takes place in Britain, nor does it affect the kind of activity which goes on in the outside world.

Since devaluation or depreciation make existing methods of production cheaper and therefore more profitable, present activities are subsidised. This staves off any need there may be to alter British production and ways of production. Thus the argument returns to the domestic scene. The balance of payments effects are certain only if the rest of the world can be persuaded always to buy the same goods from Britain. Will it always buy more British steam locomotives because they are the cheapest steam locomotives?

4 THE EFFICIENCY FUNCTION

Mass unemployment was not to recur again. On this there was general consensus after the Second World War, and on this there is still widespread consensus a generation later. The supply of money was to be regulated by the needs of trade[26] and exchange rate problems were not to stand in the way of the highest possible level of activity at home. This was achieved for the first twenty-five post-war years though there was continuous inflation. On the whole the pound sterling fulfilled its employment function, but the continuous inflation indicates this may have gone too far. Overvaluation in relation to domestic needs had given way to undervaluation in relation to domestic needs. This eventually undermined the external value of sterling and, in this sense, led to its overvaluation relative to other currencies. The term 'overvaluation' is frequently used in this sense (note, page 20). It seems inadvisable however to use the same term in two different meanings in relation to one subject. Since it is generally accepted that the pound was overvalued in the 1920s, when there was domestic unemployment and a favourable external balance, while the situation in the 1960s was one of domestic full employment with inflation and a weak external balance which was often in deficit, different terminology is required. Although the situation in the 1920s and the 1960s both eventually led to a fall in the external exchange rate so that the result was in this one respect at least the same, the causes of the fall in sterling in 1967 were entirely different from those in 1931, and so were the consequences. To use the same terminology may then obscure the true causes and the reasons for the differences in effect. In this book the value of the currency is defined in relation to domestic needs. This is not a novel way of treating the subject. It accords with some of the major post-war contributions to the subject and has for long been practised by Sir Ralph Hawtrey who has often written about monetary experience in the twentieth century without turning any definitions on their head.[27] Since the whole of twentieth-century experience is relevant to derive lessons for the 1970s, this practice will here be followed.

If it is agreed that one of the chief functions of a currency is to ensure the fullest possible utilisation of resources within its trading area, and if it is also agreed that overvaluation of the money unit effectively prevents this, then a fully employed economy cannot have an overvalued currency. It can still have a misvalued currency which does not properly fulfil its efficiency function. The currency can be undervalued. It can be too easy to earn a unit of that currency. In a sense this is always the case in times of inflation when more and more money units change hands in exchange for the same things.

Every one of us can always tell whether the value of the money unit is right or too high or too low. Just ring up your plumber and arrange for him to come on Tuesday at 12 noon. If he comes on Tuesday at 12, as many plumbers do, the value of the money unit is just right as far as your plumber is concerned. If a queue of plumbers forms outside your door on Monday, the value of the money unit is too high for your plumber and other plumbers in your area. They find it very hard to earn money and seek any kind of work that may possibly come their way. If your experience is that your plumber does not come on Tuesday at 12 (and no other plumber is in sight either) but comes a week or two later and not on a Tuesday and not at 12, then it is too easy for plumbers in your area to earn money in whatever way suits them.[28] When it is too easy to earn money work is not done on time and work is not always done properly. Although such accusations have more often been made than substantiated, and although much excellent work has been done all over the country at all times, the general impression during the first twenty-five post-war years was that 'the plumber did not come on Tuesday at 12'. Order books were full often for long periods ahead, and this bred nonchalance about what was to be produced and when. Employment seemed secure so that one could take time off for tea breaks, absenteeism and occasional strikes. Those were not days of an overvalued money unit which was too hard to get. On the contrary, such are the symptoms of an undervalued currency, when it is too easy to make a living in the good old ways and it becomes less necessary to be punctual in existing activities, let alone venture new methods of production and new goods. At such times the currency fails in its efficiency function. In this sense, it is undervalued.

The domestic remedy lies in raising the value of the money unit so that it becomes necessary to work harder and with more ingenuity in order to get better results from available (fully employed) factors of production. This means that existing activities must be replaced by better processes of production or better products or both. The remedy is not to produce cheap but to produce better. In so far as monetary measures can influence this sort of problem, the remedy is not devaluation or depreciation which makes it easier to earn money profits from existing activities. Instead the monetary remedy is appreciation of the currency which makes it more difficult to earn money in existing activities and so forces a search for new ways.

If it gets harder to earn money at home, efforts to export will be intensified. As long as full employment is maintained there are two ways of achieving this. One is to restrict home demand and so create a domestic situation as if the currency were overvalued: although full employment continues, the rewards for domestic effort in real terms are to be restricted as if there were unemployment. In practice such efforts are always resisted and usually defeated. A more promising way of raising exports is by the use of greater ingenuity. Usually this means concentrating on goods which sell on quality rather than on price or, as economists are wont to put it, goods for which demand tends to be income elastic rather than price elastic. Such goods sell best in rich and expanding markets. Goods for such markets are not likely to be 'cheap' to produce: their production requires increasing ingenuity rather than lower factor costs in existing methods of production. Production must become better rather than cheaper.

Were it only a question of the efficiency function of a currency, there might be no objection to keeping the value of the money unit as high as possible. The balance of payments was favourable in the 1920s when the pound was overvalued in relation to domestic needs but the dollar was correctly valued and some other currencies were probably undervalued.[29] The British balance of payments turned adverse in the 1930s when the dollar and other foreign currencies became overvalued in relation to *their* respective domestic needs. The British balance of payments was not as strong as hoped for in the 1950s and often adverse in the 1960s, when the pound was undervalued in relation to domestic needs. Although other countries too were worried about the maintenance of full employment and undervalued their currencies in relation to domestic needs most of that time, this appears to have gone further in Britain than elsewhere. Thus what weakens the British balance of payments is not British overvaluation but the fact that foreigners often value their money more than the British value theirs. If there is foreign overvaluation, foreigners have too little purchasing power to buy goods including British goods. It suffices, however, for the pound to be more undervalued than other major currencies, to create a situation in which it is relatively easier to sell to Britain than to sell from Britain.

None of this is an argument for raising the value of the pound sterling so much that it cannot fulfil its employment function. This would not only be regarded as intolerable but would also be self-defeating. The reason is that once a currency does not fulfil its employment function, the chief problem becomes one of how to create more employment for idle factors and not one of how to use available factors more intelligently. In Section 2 it was argued that gradual reductions in the exchange rate are preferable to drastic ones at times when the exchange rate should be lowered in order to raise the country's absolute advantage in world economic activity. The reason was that an overkill would weaken the balance of payments and so necessitate credit restraint in lieu of the credit expansion it was intended to promote. Similarly an upward revision of the exchange rate is likely to be more beneficial when it is moderate than when it is drastic. The limits it should not exceed are set by the possible rise in domestic productivity and the possible rise in world income. Given full employment, a rise in productivity implies more intelligent use of available factors. If this is not to lead to idleness of factors, purchasing power must expand sufficiently to absorb the additional goods which can now be produced. Hence the exchange rate must not rise by so much as to frustrate the appropriate credit expansion. Of course, it is not suggested that the relationship between an increase in productivity and credit expansion is mathematically precise. This varies with the commodities involved and the circumstances of the time. All that is implied is that there is a limit to which the exchange rate can safely be upvalued without impairment of the currency's employment function; and that, as long as such knowledge is imperfect and imprecise there is less risk in moving cautiously than in moving drastically.[30] The other limitation is the rise in world incomes. This matters because the exporters' money income, received in sterling, should not be reduced.

Again the relationship is neither precise nor constant. Moreover, better utilisation of factors in a fully employed industrial economy usually means the creation of more advanced goods which sell best in other industrial countries. In such countries the possible range of prices tends to be set by the prices of the nearest substitutes on sale in those various countries, plus or minus quality differential, plus the rise of incomes in those countries.[31] The limits are then set by the nature of possible advanced exports to other industrial countries and the rise of money incomes in those countries. Once again the argument points to the dangers of foreign overvaluation since that restricts foreign incomes. As long as these, admittedly imprecise, limits are observed the home currency does not become overvalued and so does not endanger its employment function if the exchange rate rises moderately.

This does not mean cheap selling. It means increasingly intelligent production. Again, this is not a law for all time. Cheap selling was possible at the beginning of the century, when the British economy had reached its technological peak for a time and was engaged in spreading its achievements throughout the world. What was wanted was known, and what was known could be produced and sold most cheaply by competitive enterprise. The attempt to restore the old world in the 1920s was in vain. Before it is possible to sell cheap (be this in itself desirable or not), it is necessary to produce cheap, and while a high exchange rate can help to keep prices down, a low one is needed to expand activity to the limits of available factors. In the post-war world, when policy makers were intent on not repeating the mistakes of the 1920s, the exchange rate was put deliberately too low in 1949 which was thought to ensure full employment irrespective of the vagaries of the balance of payments. It was meant to make more work in existing activities. It did just that. But it frustrated qualitative growth and did not even ensure the balance of payments surplus which was considered desirable at the time in order to repay war debts, raise overseas investment and add to the exchange reserves. The main reason why the low exchange rate did not lead to the hoped-for results was that, when an economy has reached such a state of maturity that it has no spare factors, the only certain result of any attempt to produce cheap is a scramble for available factors and a rise in factor prices.

The escape from such a situation lies through innovation and production with ingenuity. The problem of such an economy is not so much how to produce known goods cheaply by existing methods, but of how to produce new goods or old goods in new ways. To achieve this requires education, freer trade to allow for more international specialisation in the new goods, law and order, and much else besides a suitable monetary policy. But the absence of a suitable monetary policy can frustrate all other attempts in this direction. In the post-war years to 1968, monetary policy was deliberately relegated into the background, so as to be no more than an auxiliary to fiscal and physical controls. To some extent this may have been unavoidable. But since it always made it possible to produce 'cheap', it discouraged innovation in industry because factors of production were cheap. It also caused resentment by the factors of production which were kept 'cheap' and so led to an unending series of pay demands and pay rises which, in turn, made it increasingly impossible to produce cheap. The result was a vicious circle, in which the innovating sector of the economy was held back because it was relatively cheap to produce in traditional ways, and the traditional sector was increasingly hampered because factor prices were rising all the time. Labour was too cheap and wages were rising too fast. To labour, management seemed mean; and to management, labour seemed greedy. The situation invited strife, and it is almost miraculous that there was not more industrial unrest. What is not miraculous is that the economy grew less than it could have done, since both the innovating and the traditional sectors in each firm and throughout the industry were held back. The basic cause was the attempt to produce too cheaply when the basic situation required attempts to produce more intelligently. To produce 'too cheap' was attempted through the excessively low exchange rate fixed in 1949.

This was all-pervasive. It provides much of the explanation of why Europe's technologically most advanced economy became Europe's laggard. All expenditure on education and science, all attempts at industrial conciliation and all attempts at a successful external trading performance are frustrated if the monetary situation does not fit the real situation.

5 THE REAL SITUATION

The real economic situation in the 1950s and 1960s just did not fit the attempt at producing cheap. It did not do so at home. It did not do so internationally either. The sort of goods in which Britain once had a clear comparative advantage are the sort of goods which more and more countries have learned to produce just as well for themselves. Those countries' development has reduced the cost difference between 'beer' and 'wine' abroad, to revert to the earlier example, and this has narrowed Britain's comparative advantage in 'beer'. To pursue policies which make beer production cheaper in Britain, as for instance by means of devaluation, are an attempt to stave off the decline in Britain's comparative advantage in beer at the expense of the real incomes of the factors of production employed in beer production.

If this matter is viewed in relation to what happened in the course of the century, a better case can be made for cheap selling during much of the first half of the century than in more recent years. Throughout, Britain's comparative advantage in traditional 'beer' receded. During the first half of the century, this was most noticeable in Britain's commercial relations with already industrialised countries (and was noticeable generally in relations between the industrial countries). Because of protection, or because of lack of new ideas, or both, the already industrialised countries became more alike and the gains from trade between them receded. But this did not interfere with Britain's comparative advantage in industrial goods in her trade with the then primary producing countries. The gains from trade with those countries remained marked, and most hope for an expansion of British trade was with those countries. Since trade in primary products is largely correlated with the volume of industrial activity in the importing countries, a revival of the volume of British external trade in the 1920s and 1930s depended largely on the removal of restraint on domestic industrial activity. One major restraint was the unduly high value of the currency in the 1920s and insufficient depreciation in the 1930s. There was a case for lowering the value of the currency in the 1920s and for lowering it further in the 1930s, in order to remove that restraint and so allow for fuller activity at home and more trade with the primary producing world. That would have been beneficial. But it remains uncertain whether depreciation or more depreciation could have affected any country's comparative advantage with the world as a whole and the long-term trends in the balance of payments.

The events of the 1960s reproduced some of those problems

because of the industrialisation of the developing world. This meant, once more, waning comparative advantage in traditional industrial goods; and this time there was no Third World to which to turn where the former comparative advantage could still be utilised. The past escape, of changing the trading partners for the same trade, was no longer available. As comparative advantage was lost and sometimes even reversed (as, for instance, in certain cotton textiles), the escape lay in restructuring the home economy and specialisation in new trades. Because such change was too slow in coming, Britain's participation in world trade did not increase sufficiently to maintain her share.

Any restructuring of the British economy can be helped, or even made possible, by a reciprocal removal of tariffs between Britain and her old and new rivals. Ultimately, however, success depends on whether the economy can respond to the new international opportunities or whether it will have to turn towards a development which depends less on international trade. In either case, there will have to be less reliance on traditional industrial activities which developed in response to past comparative advantage.

The economy can respond by greater reliance on domestic primary production or by turning more and more towards increasingly complex industrial or financial activities. There are indications of a revival of primary production in Britain. Agriculture has been one of her growth activities during the last twenty-five years, the exploitation of North Sea gas has begun on a substantial scale, there are hopes for success with mineral oil and prospecting for mineral ores has revived. More British food, oil and ores would be more British primary products but they cannot be obtained by simple methods of production. The amount of capital per man in British agriculture is now comparable with that in the chemical industries.[32]

Prospecting and drilling for natural gas, mineral oil and ores requires more skills and physical capital than any but the most complex engineering activities. There may be revival and growth of primary production in Britain, but this can no longer be achieved by means of the simpler production techniques used in the past. For some time to come, a growth of British primary production will require substantial capital investment and will be in the category of increasing returns activities (on capital employed).

What applies to primary products, applies no less over the whole range of industrial activities. Since other economies have encroached upon the comparative advantage British industry once enjoyed in the production processes evolved in earlier times, and since the revival of the production of primary commodities is unlikely to provide employment for the bulk of the working population, the major escape from waning comparative advantage in present activities is through new activities in manufacturing and services. These are likely to be complex activities where the employment of pure labour per unit of output is almost certainly less than in present activities. The new activities are likely to require substantial investment in human and material capital, and if this capital is profitably invested the volume of output rises more than proportionately with the volume of additional capital input. In short, there must be factor saving in so far as less labour and capital will be needed per unit of output; and there must be increasing returns on capital employed if the required investment is put into operation and made to pay.

The domestic situation in the Britain of the 1960s was one of full employment where accelerated growth required more factor saving than was forthcoming. The external situation of Britain was one of waning comparative advantage in traditional goods. Given the rise in protection in developing countries and the tariff disarmament amongst the advanced countries, any possible increase in comparative advantage would have been in complex goods which sell best in advanced countries, including Britain. This too required more factor saving than was forthcoming, possibly because Britain did not participate as much in tariff disarmament as most other industrial countries, and possibly because her trading ties with the developing countries were exceptionally close and she was most hurt by industrialisation in those countries. Whatever the details, both the internal and the external situation pointed towards more factor saving than in fact proved possible.

Such factor saving implies increasing returns on capital employed. As output expands, unit costs of production fall until the optimum output is attained. Until then, unit costs fall relative to unit costs in all other activities taken together. The cost of 'beer' falls relative to that of 'wine' within the country. Unless there is a corresponding fall in the cost of beer abroad or a corresponding rise in the cost of wine abroad, there is an improvement in the country's comparative advantage in beer. While this indicates an improvement in the country's allocation of resources relative to the rest of the world, it does not necessarily lead to a corresponding fall in the price to the home consumer. (For as long as the good or service is produced under increasing returns, 'cheap' marginal cost pricing is impossible since average cost exceeds marginal cost. The price to the consumer remains above marginal cost and may remain constant over a wide range of production.) A fall in unit cost, with a less than proportionate fall in price, or no fall in price, means that profits per unit produced rise. This encourages an expansion of production. In times of full employment, this may be the only way in which one activity can expand relative to others. While the law of comparative costs is as valid when production takes place under conditions of increasing returns as under any other production conditions, under conditions of increasing returns comparative advantage tends to reveal itself not so much in prices charged to consumers as in unit profits earned by producers. It becomes a *law of comparative profits*.

The real situation of the 1950s and 1960s thus required more efficiency rather than more employment. A low exchange rate, however, is more conducive to more employment than to greater efficiency. When there are idle machines and unwanted men the problem is how to produce more known goods with existing equipment and men of given skills. Re-employment can be facilitated by a lowering of the exchange rate and credit expansion, because this helps to produce cheap which, in turn, makes it possible to sell cheap. The economy then gains an absolute advantage but, if the rest of the world retaliates, this can lead to commercial conflict with other countries. They may be plagued by similar problems and seek more absolute advantage for themselves. In such circumstances each country protects itself, for instance, by means of lower exchange rate in order to make more work for its own people. More people can work or all may work more in order to get the same assortment of goods as before but without benefit of international specialisation. The latter is unwanted because it reduces the amount of work needed for the same result. Falling exchange rates are then part of the armoury of economic nationalism and since this also means a debasement of the government's domestic monetary command, it tends to go hand in hand with an increase in the central government's exercise of direct physical power. This re-statement of the position in inter-war days should suffice to show how far removed all this was from the world of the 1950s and 1960s and from British economic interests at that time.

In the 1950s and until the late 1960s sterling fulfilled its employment function. If monetary policy failed in any way in those two decades, it was because it did not make urgent the need to become more efficient through more intelligent use of factors. To be fair, this was not what the policy makers of the immediate post-war period set out to do. Economists and public opinion generally demanded full employment. This was achieved. The loss was in qualitative growth through factor saving. There was less change in the variety and quality of goods and services than might have been technologically possible. Since the Third World industrialises and pins its hopes on import substitution at the expense of Britain's known goods, and since the advanced industrial countries increasingly specialise amongst themselves and on new rather than known goods, hopes for a better export performance in known goods were often disappointed. Most of the new goods sell on quality rather than on price. But the low exchange rate policy of 1949 and after was based on the assumption that price was the most important consideration—as it usually is with known goods.

Grumbles about economic performance in the 1950s and 1960s should not be taken too far. Except for the last years of the 1960s and the very start of the 1970s, the employment position was satisfactory, the growth of gross domestic product of the British economy was high by its own historic standards and so was the growth of exports. It was not the case that the British economy did badly but rather that other industrial economies did even better in terms of growth though not necessarily in terms of employment. This was at least in part due to the policy pursued. The emphasis on the employment function of the currency was deliberate, and it took time to become apparent that the policy's very success impaired the efficiency of the economy. Even if this is not the whole explanation, there is a direct link between the policy objectives of the time, the balance of payments and why the plumber did not come on Tuesday at 12.

4

Chapter Two　THE EFFECTS OF
DEVALUATION
IN 1967

I THE POOR

In November 1967 the pound was devalued by 14·3 per cent. This means values expressed in sterling represent that much less in terms of United States dollars, and values expressed in United States dollars represent 16·7 per cent more in terms of sterling.

Some hoped that devaluation would be a cure for the balance of payments problems which had beset the British economy in the 1960s, when credit was intermittently kept tight and a miscellany of other controls were applied to restrain domestic spending in order to release goods for export. Such measures had been taken in the hope of curing balance of payments deficits though at the price of domestic restraint. This had happened in 1960, in 1964 and again in mid 1966, and in each case there was an improvement in the balance of payments within three to fifteen months later.[1] But each time domestic restraint had adverse effects on the growth of output for the home market or for any market, so that some commentators came to be reminded of the 1920s when the economy was kept in shackles for the sake of an unduly high exchange rate. Far better, so the argument ran, to let the exchange rate go and with it all the restraints that had been imposed to support it.

Such views were not held unanimously. The authorities themselves resisted devaluation as long as they could. The arguments which may or may not have swayed them were no doubt manifold, ranging from the political odium that seemed to be attached to any exchange rate variation in the 1960s to consideration for the poor at home and the poorer countries of the sterling area abroad. For it is the poor at home and abroad who have to bear the brunt of such adjustment.

The poor at home were especially vulnerable since the proportion of their incomes that is spent on food is particularly large and, under the agricultural policy of the time, British market prices were set by import prices.[2] It has been possible to ignore such considerations in 1931[3] when many overseas supplying countries tied their currencies to sterling and others let their exchange rates drop even more, so that there were then no adverse welfare effects of this nature. It was still possible to put such considerations second to the expectations relating to employment and the balance of payments in 1949, when nearly all overseas sterling area countries followed sterling exactly[4] and the majority of other non-dollar countries also devalued though most of them by less. When sterling was devalued again in 1967, of the major supplying countries only New Zealand and Ceylon devalued by more, and only Denmark and the Caribbean Commonwealth countries followed sterling exactly. This provided considerable relief since New Zealand supplies much of British dinners, Denmark breakfasts, Ceylon tea and the Caribbean the sugar that goes with it. But the majority of countries did not devalue and this included a large number of sterling area countries. One consequence was that when world food prices fell by 3 per cent in 1968 British food import prices rose by 5 per cent.[5] This was unusual because normally British food import prices and world food prices move in the same direction and the difference in 1968 was directly attributable to the devaluation of sterling. During the following two years world food prices rose by 3 per cent a year and British food prices moved in the same direction but by more. To be precise, they rose by 5 per cent. Not all of this can be attributed to devaluation, but some of it must have been due to delayed adjustment in import prices since food imports are often contracted for a long period ahead. Moreover, it takes time for a rise in import prices to be reflected in the shops. For a time traders could sell from stocks, and there was slower adjustment in the cost of domestic distribution and packaging than in the price of the food content. But, for the poor especially, it is the price of the food content that matters. In any case the rise in prices did eventually percolate through the system.

Although this carries the narrative somewhat ahead of what happened in 1967, the longer term effects on food have been singled out for first attention because they meant a complete break with the past. At the beginning of the century, British prosperity had depended upon cheap imports which, in turn, had depended upon a strong currency. In the 1930s, when the currency was weak, free trade in food was abandoned. Food supplies from overseas could no longer be relied on so much when the currency had become weaker—and ever since the debate has not been whether there should be protection of home agriculture but rather what sort of protection for home agriculture there should be. In the 1930s protection took the form of import quotas and the introduction of marketing boards which were meant to safeguard the prices received by home producers. But in the 1930s prices were so low, and overseas suppliers were still so willing to oblige the British market, that 'cheap food' was dented rather than abandoned. The policy adopted in the late 1940s was one of allowing import prices of food to set domestic market prices and to subsidise home farmers by paying them the 'deficiency' between their average realised market prices and the target prices negotiated between the National Farmers Union and the Ministry of Agriculture. 'Cheap food' was still papered over and its welfare effects maintained, but at the expense of the taxpayer and no longer by means of a strong currency. Although the system of deficiency payments was continued as a form of agricultural support for some time longer and only began to be replaced by an import levy system from 1971 onwards, the pretence of cheap food was gone with the devaluation of 1967.

In 1968 the volume of food imports rose at nearly the 1967 rate of 3 per cent, when much of it must have been contracted for before the devaluation. But it fell back by a similar amount in 1969. It stayed at the 1967 level in 1969 and 1970. Even in 1968, the share of food in total imports fell back. It was to be lower from that time onwards than it had been at any time from the abolition of the Corn Laws to the 1967 devaluation.[6]

As far as food was concerned, the devaluation could be adjudged a 'success' since it stabilised food imports at a time when imports in general were not at all stable. At the same time, consumption was also stable although the population continued to rise at the normal rate. There was not so much diversion of demand from imports to domestic sources of supplies as some decline in household consumption. The reason is quite simply that prices mattered to the housewife and especially the poorer one who buys the cheaper cuts of meat and the cheaper butter, most of which are imported.

If the poor at home could not evade some of the consequences of devaluation, the poorer countries in the overseas sterling area could not do so either. Countries were in the sterling area if they kept the bulk of their exchange reserves in sterling. Like all countries, they regulated their domestic money supply so as not to endanger the possibility of converting the national money into international means of exchange. In their case, this meant sterling.

As long as development in those countries depended largely on British lending and British trade, sterling was the ideal reserve currency for them. But in the 1950s and 1960s British trade grew less than the trade of other industrial countries, and this somewhat weakened the trading ties between Britain and sterling area countries. More important was the persistent British balance of payments weakness in the 1960s which reduced the volume of net lending which Britain could sustain. Overseas sterling area countries had to look increasingly elsewhere for external funds and, on the whole, the economically stronger sterling area countries were more successful in this respect than the weaker ones. Nonetheless most of the external debt of those countries remained a sterling debt, and this was expected to continue. (This belief was shattered in June 1972, when Britain applied exchange controls on capital exports to the sterling area and so weakened the most important monetary link with the area.)

The attraction of basing a country's currency on the currency of the chief lender is that it eases the repayments problem. A sterling area country can repay a sterling debt out of export earnings or out of earnings arising from increased domestic activity which are ultimately convertible into sterling. It can repay a dollar debt only out of export earnings. As long as the bulk of indebtedness is in sterling and is likely to remain so, such countries may wish to remain in the sterling area. But as external borrowing is increasingly done in dollars and other non-sterling currencies, it pays them to diversify their exchange reserves in order to minimise the risk of their own default.

As long as sterling maintains its exchange value, there is no further problem. If sterling is devalued, as it was in 1967, the sterling content of these countries' exchange reserves is correspondingly reduced in value. In so far as their sterling holdings are largely holdings to ensure debt redemption, it may not matter to them externally. But their sterling holdings are also used as backing for their national money, and a devaluation of sterling then forces domestic deflation upon them. To counter this they may have to devalue as well, only to find that this weakens their purchasing power and trade with third countries. In consequence, a devaluation of sterling 'succeeds' in cutting off dependent currency countries from alternative trading partners.

If the rate of those countries' domestic inflation after devaluation is the same as in Britain, there may seem to be no further adverse effects on their trade with Britain. But this may be an illusion. The immediate effect is almost bound to be adverse. The reason is that, in such countries, control of national money supply is more closely linked to their exchange reserves than is the case in Britain, and those exchange reserves were devalued. Hence there are monetary difficulties which adversely affect those countries' activity and total trade. It follows that the most Britain can hope for in sterling area trade, after devaluation, is a larger share in a smaller volume of trade.

A number of sterling area countries have diversified their exchange reserves for some time and it is a measure of their increasing monetary independence that many of them felt able to maintain their dollar exchange parities at the time of the 1967 sterling devaluation. This applied to Australia, India, Pakistan and the major African countries.[7] For them there was still loss of exchange reserves and some deflation effect, but the loss affected only some of their exchange reserves. Hence their loss of purchasing power was mitigated. Nonetheless there was some loss and even in their case Britain could only hope for a larger share of a smaller trade than there would have been in the absence of devaluation. In fact, the share of the sterling area in Britain's export trade continued to decline after devaluation just as much as it had done before devaluation, and probably at a larger rate than would have happened without devaluation. This had not been so apparent in 1949. Then, most overseas sterling area countries had money balances accumulated in return for supplying Britain during the war. After the 1949 devaluation had reduced the dollar value of those balances, they could still be used to buy British goods and so maintain supplies within the various overseas sterling area countries. This was of importance until the late 1950s, when there were few sterling balances left other than those needed for monetary and trading requirements.[8] By 1967, however, there was no cushion of wartime sterling balances to work off.

In short, at home and in the overseas sterling area, devaluation could and did succeed at the expense of the weakest members in the sterling community.

2 THE WORKERS

Devaluation hurts the poor especially because it hangs the bread basket higher. But none are entirely immune from its consequences. All must work harder for the same standard of living as before. There is more work to go round. Production is now cheap in terms of money units and this makes it possible to employ more people. Since production is cheaper, there is less need to alter methods of production. There is more work for more people in the economy as it is.

Nowadays this is widely accepted as beneficial when there is not enough work to go round, since it seems better that more work be done to achieve the same overall result than that men should be unwanted in the economy. Moreover there is always the hope that the higher money incomes received by producers and those previously on the dole, may have favourable multiplier effects. In 1967, however, there was still enough work to go round. Put differently, the level of employment was still high. True, at the time of devaluation the unemployment rate was slightly over 2 per cent, and this was somewhat higher than the $1\frac{1}{2}$ per cent which had prevailed in most of the

1950s and 1960s until 1966.[9] But about a quarter of the 1967 unemployment rate may be attributed to longer intervals between jobs.[10] This has been made possible by the introduction of redundancy payments for dismissed workers in 1965 and earnings-related social security benefits for those temporarily out of work in 1966. Thus, the devaluation came at a time of high employment. A major rise in unemployment was not to occur until the 1970s.

Even if the rise in unemployment in 1967 could be regarded as an indication of the availability of more spare factors, a 14·3 per cent devaluation would seem to be a drastic way of dealing with an increase of unemployment of less than one per cent. Altogether there was no reason for a 14·3 per cent real wage cut in order to spread the work load. There would have been such a reason only if the country had been at an absolute disadvantage in using its resources. But unemployment was higher in the United States, ranging at the time somewhere between $3\frac{1}{2}$ and 4 per cent.

A devaluation of sterling cuts the real rewards of all British factors relative to factors in all other countries. Nevertheless the argument will proceed largely in terms of wages and in terms of the relationship between sterling values and dollar values. The reasons for concentrating on wages will be dealt with first. They are twofold.

One reason is that British technology can be said to have been less productive and, in this sense, inferior to American technology at the time of devaluation. It is also possible to say that higher education was not as widespread in Britain as in the United States. But it is not possible to say that British basic education (or any other education for that matter) was inferior to American education. Against this background the effects of devaluation appear as follows. The lower exchange rate meant not only a lower value of the currency but of all that the currency represents. This means all current values created in Britain and consequently the worth of all factors which create these values. A devaluation of the currency thus means a flat devaluation of the worth of British capital and British labour. If British capital was inferior to American and British labour was not, a flat devaluation of British factors then penalised British labour relatively more and less deservedly.

The second reason for concentrating on wages is that a wage is the reward for current labour. Since all economic activity involves a current effort, there is a wage element in the reward for any economic activity. But the importance of that wage element varies. The earnings which are nearest to pure wages are the rewards received by operatives on the factory floor. It is customary to refer to them as 'the wage earners'. Others also receive wages but the wage element is less. For instance, salary earners work currently and this entitles them to a wage but they receive more than a wage. Most of them have education beyond the minimal secondary modern education everybody gets, and these special skills acquired in the past give them an 'educational rent' in addition to a wage for current effort. Profits are the rewards for entrepeneurship which includes both a wage and a salary element as well as some reward for uncertainty bearing. Rent is a return derived from ownership of property acquired in the past, but since the collection of such rent involves some current effort, rent actually received includes at least some wage element. Thus there is a wage element in the rewards for all economic activities, but this element varies from being the predominant one in the case of operatives to being negligible in the case of rent. Since devaluation of the British currency lowers the worth of current British activities and so devalues British wages, it penalises British operatives most and British property owners least.[11]

Before this point is developed, there must be a few words

about why the argument concentrates on the relation between sterling values and dollar values. In the past, the value of sterling was expressed in gold and any change in the gold parity reflected changes in British values relative to world values. The post-war devaluations were in terms of the United States dollar, and only the United States dollar had a direct gold value. This reflected the central position of the United States in the world economy of the time, when other countries expressed the value of their currencies in dollars and adjusted their exchange rates in terms of dollars. The dollar was the world's chief currency, and currency reserves were held in dollars or in gold because gold was convertible into dollars. There may come a time when the dollar will no longer occupy such a central position but this was not so in 1967. At that time, an adjustment of the sterling exchange rate was in terms of dollars and this meant an adjustment of sterling values relative to dollar values. That adjustment of values included a cut of British real wages relative to United States wages. It also implied a cut of British wages and values relative to other countries' wages and values. But these too were influenced by their dollar exchange rates. The relationship between, say, sterling and franc values depended on the exchange rate of each with the dollar. There was a cut in British relative to French wages only if the dollar value of sterling fell while the dollar value of the franc remained unchanged.

Some of the principal effects of the devaluation of sterling in 1967 can then be reviewed in terms of what happened to British relative to American wages. Devaluation disturbs existing trading relationships and, whenever there is a disturbance to international trade, such trade must be 'resumed' under the new conditions. Of course trade goes on all the time, the day before devaluation and the day after devaluation and all days before and since. Nevertheless the conditions of trade have changed. When this happens, the existing relationship between prices is disturbed, but the 'resumption' of trade means that there will be tendencies for product and factor prices to revert towards their former relationship. Trade makes product prices more equal in the various trading countries than would be the case in the absence of trade. Where trade is free, as for instance between London and Exeter, the traveller from either town to the other knows in advance what prices will be like in the shops. Any differences there are tend to be slight and can usually be explained by transport costs. The traveller to New York cannot be so sure of what prices of various goods will be like since he goes to a different tariff and monetary area. But as trade increases between Britain and the United States, the price differences become less even if they do not altogether disappear. If the pound is devalued relative to the dollar, these price differences become larger, but this cannot last indefinitely unless Britain cuts herself off from trade with the United States.

Once product prices tend towards equality, there is bound to be some effect on the rewards payable to the factors used in their production. Factor rewards, too, become more equal, though these tendencies may face even greater obstacles than the tendencies towards product price equalisation and manifest themselves less clearly. Nevertheless they operate and are likely to be least slow for factors whose rewards include a large wage element and slowest for those whose rewards contain only a small wage element.[12] Again these tendencies are likely to be least slow for factors most directly engaged in production for export, or can most easily be transferred to such production. Factors most easily transferred are those least specific to their present employment, and this again means mostly those whose earnings contain a large wage element. In other words, these tendencies are most likely to show up in the case of wage-labour engaged in the production of exportable goods which, in Britain's case, means largely manufactures. It does not follow that exportables are necessarily exported. The production of the same goods for export and for home consumption cannot easily be separated and cannot be rewarded differently. All that follows is a tendency towards a general rise in wages throughout manufacturing industry. If devaluation has made labour 'cheap', any subsequent trade and trade expansion makes it 'dear' again.

After 1967, it took approximately four years for British labour to become as dear again as it had been in 1967. This took the form of a greater rise in British than American wages. The details will be shown below. But first let it be considered why this could not be averted after 1967. Devaluation makes labour cheap and trade expansion makes it dear. Had trade stagnated and unemployment risen, there would have been no such rise in wages. But it was no one's intention that trade should stagnate and no one's intention that unemployment should rise. It was believed that devaluation would raise exports. Earlier in the year the Kennedy Round of tariff negotiations under the General Agreement on Tariffs and Trade had come to a successful conclusion, so that there was further ground for hope of trade expansion. British exports had stagnated in 1967 and world exports had grown somewhat less than usual in that year, but both resumed their upward course in 1968. A curtailment of trade is wanted only in times of unemployment, which are also the sort of times in which a devaluation can help to raise the level of employment in existing activities and at prevailing money wage rates.

In times of trade expansion, this is not possible. Production tends to be reorganised to meet the rising international demand as profitably as possible. Factors of production then gravitate towards employments most suited to meet this demand and, not unnaturally, expect rewards similar to those prevailing

internationally at current exchange rates. Devaluation inter-
rupts this process. Because it makes current labour relatively
cheap, there is less need to reorganise production as long as
labour stays cheap. But labour will stay cheap only if at least
one of the two conditions mentioned before is satisfied. One is
that there is so much unemployment at home that an increase
in the demand for labour does not drive up the wage rate. No
one knows for certain how large the volume of unemployment
must be to satisfy this condition, but a widely respected
estimate puts it at $5\frac{1}{2}$ per cent or more.[18] This condition was not
satisfied in 1967. Nor was the alternative condition, which is
stagnation or decline in world trade. This would have removed
the outside pressures towards the reorganisation of activities
and higher factor rewards. But the sharp revival of world trade
in 1968 meant that these pressures were intensified. Factor
prices rose appropriately and became less cheap, and this was
particularly marked in respect of current labour which had
been most penalised by devaluation. This movement was not
sudden. As already mentioned, it took about four years.

The devaluation gain, if it was a gain, to British producers
was that profits rose temporarily without the need for reorganisation. As long as labour was cheap, there was less need
for factor saving and therefore for new investment. Surplus
funds which could have been used to finance new investments
were diverted to attract cheap labour, with the result that labour
ceased to be cheap. Instead of investment and the prospect for
accelerated growth, there was a futile scramble for factors
coupled with stagnation of the nature of British economic
activities.

Much of this will be the subject matter of section 3 below.
Here it must suffice to see what happened to wages. It will be
recalled that the 1967 devaluation was one of 14·3 per cent in
terms of the dollar. The preceding has shown that this meant a

flat cut in current earnings which hurt wage-labour most, partly because wage-labour most truly reflects the reward for current toil, and partly because any inferiority of British relative to American factors was an overall inferiority in capital equipment rather than of labour. The 14·3 per cent fall in the exchange rate is then only an approximate indication of the devaluation of British labour. Since the overall devaluation affected other factors less, it may be an underestimate.

The 14·3 per cent fall in the exchange rate must be accepted as the nearest indication there is. The wage element in any £100 earned fell to £85·70 at the old exchange rate. At a time of high employment and trade expansion, it unleashed tendencies towards an equilibrating rise in British relative to American wages. To move back from £85·70 to £100 at the new exchange rate, meant a rise of 16·7 per cent in British relative to American wages.

A comparison of earnings in United States manufacturing establishments[14] and the average earnings of male labour in British manufacturing industry,[15] in October each year, shows the following changes. Starting with October 1967, the month before devaluation, British wages had risen 8 per cent more than American wages by October 1970, and 17 per cent more by October 1971.[16] By the time of writing, it is known the British wages continued to rise sharply in the first half of 1972. Was it that the rise in the previous years was habit-forming or was it that a somewhat further excess rise of British over American wages was still to follow to equilibrate the 1967 exchange rate? By that time, however, the exchange rate had risen to $2·60 in December 1971—though this higher rate was abandoned in June 1972, largely because of the disquiet caused by 'inflationary' wage settlements.

It is not yet possible to pass judgement. Perhaps the 'wage explosion' of the late 1960s and early 1970s had really become an explosion in so far as it forced the exchange rate down (in June 1972) rather than followed the exchange rate (as from 1967 to 1971). If so, then the 1967 Anglo-American wage parity must have been right. This is by no means certain. It may have been too high or too low then. The pound was devalued in 1939 and although British wages rose less than American wages during the next ten years,[17] it was devalued again in 1949. Subsequently British wages rose more than American wages and this restored the 1949 wage parity by about 1967,[18] when there was another devaluation. Throughout, the rise in wages raised costs of production in existing activities which presented a choice of protecting those activities by a cut in real wages through a lowering of the exchange rate or to encourage factor-saving investment.

Whether the path chosen was right or wrong, any time there is a devaluation when trade expands, it sets in motion equilibrating price movements which are most clearly marked in the case of wages. Hence, whoever willed the $2·40 exchange rate in 1967, also willed the wage explosion after 1967.

3 INDUSTRY

The wage explosion did not only apply to the earnings of operatives. Rather it meant that there was a rise in the wage element every economically active person gets for the time spent at work and for the basic secondary modern skills, *relative* to the higher skills and *relative* to risk and uncertainty bearing. This situation reflects retarded growth where, whatever may happen in individual activities, the overall picture is one of sameness. As will be shown below, there is not even change in the share of labour in national income. There just is no change.

The distribution of factor earnings is a reflection of the sort

5

of employment the economy provides, and this in itself reflects some aspects of industrial structure. The apparent paradox of labour being too cheap and wages rising too fast is a reflection of the way a devaluation influences the devaluing country's industrial structure. The initial effect of devaluation is that it makes British labour relatively cheap, with the result that firms plan to use more labour relative to other factors. Production becomes more a matter of current toil and less one of skill or capital utilisation. In times of under-utilised capital and unemployed labour, this is just what is wanted. It was possible to commend this in the 1930s and to regret the depreciation had not gone further so that there might have been more employment in industry as it then was. In 1967 there was little scope for further employment. Devaluation still made British labour relatively cheap and since nearly all British labour was already employed, this just meant a scramble for labour and a disregard for factor-saving innovations.

This does not mean to say that managements were not aware of opportunities for factor-saving innovations, but these usually require initial investment. As labour costs were low it seemed less necessary to invest and investment plans were always inadequate. But as labour costs always rose by more than anticipated, there just were not the funds to meet all of the investment plans. To stress the point once more: because labour was cheap, investment plans were inadequate; and because labour costs were rising, the already inadequate investment plans could not be met.

Although the cost of wage-labour rose, the share of wage-labour in national income did not rise. That share had been 40 per cent in the three years preceding devaluation. It was $38\frac{1}{2}$ per cent in 1968, 39 per cent in 1969 and $39\frac{1}{2}$ per cent in 1970.[19] The share of labour in national income has fluctuated around 40 per cent throughout the last hundred years and the variation in the late 1960s was not unusual.[20] A fall below 40 per cent has frequently occurred before, especially in times of recession; and the late 1960s were years of stagnation. The mere fact that the share of wages did not rise at a time of rising labour costs seems to reflect the fact that the opportunities for growth through the employment of more labour were rather limited. Wages just rose with money incomes. Wage rates went up, but the share of wage-labour in the national income did not. Devaluation favoured growth based on wage-labour. There was no spare wage-labour, next to no growth—just a rise in prices.

Wages reflect the reward for current toil better than do any other factor rewards; while salaries include not only a reward for current toil but also a reward for skills acquired in the past. These skills are normally at a higher level than those obtained in the sort of secondary modern education most wage earners have. Moreover, while wage earners perform the immediate tasks which create values on completion of the task in hand, salary earners are more concerned with decisions that determine what values will be created in the future. This applies to the salaried Prime Minister, business executive and draughtsman. It also applies to their typists whose work has no immediate value but becomes valuable when the letters, memoranda or whatever else they may have typed are read and acted upon. That is why the wage earners' tasks are the tasks of today, while the salary earners' tasks are the tasks performed with the skills of yesterday and a view to tomorrow. Thus wage earners are rewarded for current toil and salary earners for current toil plus special skills. If then there is a change in the relative rewards received by wage and salary earners, this reflects a change in the toil content and the skill content of current activity (where toil refers to the creation of current values, and skill to the creation of future values).

In this respect there is conflicting evidence from what happened in the economy as a whole and what happened in manufacturing industry. The share of salaries in national income has been rising steadily from the mid-1950s onwards, which was the time when the first beneficiaries of the 1944 Education Act entered the labour market. As they move up the various salary scales and as new entrants come on to the market each year, the share of salaries in national income rises. In the absence of further educational changes, this can be expected to continue until the late 1990s when the first beneficiaries of wider and higher educational opportunities are due to retire. This basic situation is unlikely to be directly affected by any currency changes. It can yet be modified by opportunities in manufacturing industry and other activities which are directly influenced by changes in relative values of labour at home and abroad.

An indication of what happens to the relative toil content and skill content of current activity is given by what happens to the average wage and average salary in various activities. (Unfortunately it is not possible to calculate this for the economy as a whole since the total number of people employed in salary-earning occupations and wage-earning occupations is available for census years only. At the time of writing the last available census data relate to 1961 and the 1971 census will not be available for some time yet.) Details are however available for the totals of salaries and wages paid in manufacturing industry and the numbers employed as salary and wage earners in manufacturing industry. When the total salary bill is divided by the number of salary earners and the same is done for the total wages bill and the number of wage earners in manufacturing industry, it is possible to see what happened to the average industrial salary and the average industrial wage. The result is as follows.

In the 1950s and in the 1960s until 1967, the average industrial wage took about seven to eight years to catch up the average industrial salary.[21] For instance in 1950 the average industrial salary was £508 a year and the average industrial wage in 1957 was £503 and in 1958 it was £525. In 1951 the average industrial salary was £544, in 1958 the average industrial wage £525 and in 1959 £548. This was quite a regular feature of the industrial scene. It was slightly delayed only in 1963, when an exceptionally cold winter hit wage earners harder than salary earners and it took somewhat over eight years for the average industrial wage to catch up with average industrial salary. But, 1963 apart, it could be said that there was a seven to eight years' lag between salaries and wages. This applied until 1967. The average industrial salary in 1959 had been £831; in 1966 the average industrial wage £814 and in 1967 £846. This regularity was broken after 1967. In 1968, the average industrial wage had advanced to £916 which is between the average salary of 1961 (£905) and 1962 (£940), this being a lag of only six to seven years. In 1969, the average industrial wage had gone up to £985 which is between the average salary of 1963 (£982) and 1964 (£1,047). This was a lag of between only five to six years, though rather close to six years. In 1970, the average industrial wage was £1,108 which is between the average salary of 1965 (£1,047) and 1966 (£1,121). Hence the lag was only between four and five years.

This shortening of the time lag may be interpreted in different ways. Much play has been made of trade union power[22] but this poses the question of why trade unions should have become more powerful around 1967. Others may point to differences in the rate of inflation which accelerated after 1967. But the rate of inflation had not been regular before 1967, while the seven to eight years' lag of the average industrial wage behind the average industrial salary had been regular.

There seems to be no satisfactory answer without reference to the devaluation which gave inflation a special slant towards 'wage explosion'. For devaluation had made current British toil cheap relative to American, and this led to an equilibrating movement. Until such a movement is complete, labour remains cheap. There is less demand for the skills required for planning ahead and more demand for current toil. As long as this lasts, change is discouraged and industry stands still. Although industry did not stand entirely still, it went through a phase of low growth and low investment. The acceleration of the rise in wage earnings relative to salary earnings is an indication that manufacturing industry lived more for today and had less thought for tomorrow than in the years before 1967.

To care more for today and less for tomorrow is often right. It may be better to seek an absolute advantage for what there is rather than to produce more intelligently. This was so in the inter-war years when increasing protectionism throughout the industrial world blocked the avenues towards more inter-national specialisation. In such circumstances it may be pre-ferable to let the exchange rate go if this enables the credit expansion needed for the re-employment of idle men in empty factories. But such retreat into re-employment was not necessary in 1967. True there was stagnation in British exports in that year and world trade grew somewhat less than it usually did in the 1960s. But world trade soon resumed a marked upward trend. At home there were few spare factors. Britain's chief need was to raise her comparative advantage through more efficient use of resources, and the best prospects for that pro-bably lay in increased intra-industry specialisation[23]—which means international specialisation between firms within the same industry. This requires skills at a par with the highest in the advanced industrial world. The rise in the reward for the toil content of industrial activity is hardly a way of encouraging such specialisation.

Such specialisation can develop its full potential only in times of marked economic growth. As it was, devaluation hit an economy that just seemed to be on the verge of expansion. A regular feature in British economic experience in the twentieth century has been that a rise in the real national income is preceded by a rise in money profits.[24] At the time of devaluation, the economy just seemed to recover from a period of sluggishness. Profits were rising again and there was some increase in real income in 1968. But this was not maintained. Profits fell back and so did the gross domestic product at constant factor cost. The latter rose by 2·1 per cent in 1969, 1·2 per cent in 1970, and from the third quarter of 1970 to the third quarter of 1971 it once more seemed to recover to about 2·4 per cent. But this was not enough, given the technological possibilities of the day and given the fact that such a slowly growing economy cannot maintain the level of employment. In general once the rate of growth falls much under $2\frac{1}{2}$ per cent, unemployment tends to rise. But no greater growth was possible as long as more was paid for doing what was done before.

In sum, devaluation confers an absolute advantage on existing activities and, if there are no spare factors available for existing activities, the economy stands still. When there are no spare factors, growth depends on factor saving which, in turn, usually means reorganisation and investment. The cost of such reorganisation and investment can be recouped only after the sale of goods it had helped to create. If few units of output are sold, the capital cost per unit produced is high; but if many are sold, such cost is low. With rising output, there are increasing returns on capital employed. The situation created by devaluation is however inimical to reorganisation, investment and increasing returns. The declining premium on skill, relative to toil, discourages the reorganisation men. The cheapness of labour dulls managements into a false sense of security that existing ways can continue. The rising cost of labour makes it more difficult to find the funds for new investment. Old activities continue, first by choice and later of necessity. Since old activities are activities which continue without reorganisation and new investment, their expansion means that their equipment is used to capacity which often implies rising unit costs (or diminishing returns). Within each firm and in consequence throughout the economy, diminishing returns activities survive longer and increasing returns activities start later, and for both reasons there are higher costs per unit produced. This applies even without reference to the scramble for factors as each activity seeks to gain or retain factors.

An unduly low value of money thus raises costs and ensures the survival of the antiquated rather than the fittest. Graduates and executives are needed less. As the 1960s drew to a close increasing numbers of them faced unemployment: one wonders how many of them owed this fate to devaluation.

Nor did devaluation protect the wage-earning population from unemployment, the way one used to think (quite correctly) in the 1920s and 1930s. For every executive or graduate in industrial employment, there were about three wage earners assisting him.[25] For a time the employment risks to wage earners are papered over by apparently cheap labour but as the equilibrating rise in wages gathers more momentum and finally equilibrium is attained, first in one activity, then in another and then all round, cheap labour ceases. Less skilled labour is then no longer an alternative to more highly skilled labour even in a stagnant economy. Both get their dismissals.

Economists know by now how to avoid the mass unemployment which was entrenched by the overvaluations of the currency in the 1920s and 1930s. In order to avoid the mistakes of those days, post-war policy swung to the other extreme and kept the exchange rate too low. This underwrote the *status quo* in industry and other economic activities. It may have been a lesser error to undervalue than to overvalue but there was still misvaluation. Any misvaluation stops the economy from moving and so eventually threatens employment. This applies equally whether the misvaluation be an overvaluation which puts the exchange rate too high or whether it be an under-valuation which puts it too low. But while overvaluation does this by undermining the traditional sector which is the bulk of the economy and therefore more immediately noticeable, undervaluation does this by undermining the growth sector which may account for no more than a few per cent of the economy but determines its direction in the future. That sector depends upon graduates and executives. They become less wanted as the economy grows less. As they are less wanted, the wage earners who assist them are also less wanted.

4 THE BALANCE OF PAYMENTS

The dire domestic consequences of devaluation are a commercial penalty. If the punishment is to fit the crime, this penalty fits a situation where the commercial balance of payments is chronically weak because the people in the currency area do not produce as much as they could but make up for the difference by consuming more of what is produced abroad. Eventually such people must suffer a cut in their external purchasing power. They get it through a fall in the exchange rate of their currency. To argue from this that *any* fall in the exchange rate is an indication of spendthrift commercial incompetence of the economy which had to devalue its currency flies in the face of much twentieth-century experience. Nevertheless such scolding of the British commercial community has become so commonplace that it is widely almost accepted as a fact. Yet none of the falls of sterling was due to such a cause. Sterling fell in 1931 after a period when the British did not spend enough at home or abroad and were eventually driven off an unduly high exchange rate when overseas customers ceased to spend as much as before. The devaluation of 1939 can be attributed to wartime relations with the United States. The 1949 devaluation was a deliberate devaluation to avoid a feared post-war slump which was expected to originate in the United States where incomes were expected to fall. What happened in 1967?

1967 saw the culmination of balance of payments difficulties which had threatened for some time. They had surfaced in 1964, when the balance of payments on current account showed a deficit of £376 million (which had previously been exceeded or nearly equalled only in 1947 and 1951, with £381 million and £369 million respectively).[26] Despite all efforts to prevent a recurrence and despite some success in 1965 and 1966, there was another substantial deficit in 1967—this time of £298 million.

The recurrent balance of payments weakness in the mid-1960s reflected the cumulative effects of weaknesses in the general economic situation which were indicated in previous sections. There it was shown that, in the post-war period, more attention was paid to the employment function of sterling than to its efficiency function. This made the economy rely unduly on the employment of labour in existing activities and not enough on the investment needed to create new activities in place of the old ones. The result was that Britain offered for export a more antiquated assortment of goods than might have been possible—and this was not helpful towards greater export success at a time when the growth of world trade was most marked in specialised manufactures which sell more on quality than on price. In so far as this situation was capable of being remedied by devaluation, it depended on greater trading opportunities with the Third World where the older goods still sell and price considerations are overriding. But any such attempts would seem to run counter to the policies of many of those countries which, rightly or wrongly, seek development through import substitution. This applied in 1967 as it does now.

Devaluation may help, or force, a country to make more use of what equipment it has. Recurrent balance of payments deficits may also force a country to do so and devaluation may be the means chosen. A balance of payments deficit means that the country currently imports more than it pays for with its exports. Effectively it relies on overseas savings. This means that the country imports capital. Such capital can consist of purely monetary accommodation which may be suitable for tiding over temporary balance of payments difficulties. It may also mean monetary help towards the purchase of investment goods which is more appropriate to offset the inadequacy of home investment. If neither monetary accommodation nor help towards the purchase of investment goods is available, the country cannot have a balance of payments deficit but must make do with what it has. Towards that end, devaluation helps. The 'punishment' of lower real incomes for those who work today seems to fit the 'crime' of not having invested more yesterday.

The authorities strove to avert this punishment in 1964 and managed to stave it off for three years. Market forces were not in their favour, though as recently as 1960 market forces had made a substantial deficit (of £255 million) innocuous.[27] On that occasion, there was an inflow of private funds which exceeded the deficit. As long as overseas residents acquire sterling securities worth at least as much as the deficit, be those sterling securities titles to real assets or bank deposits denominated in sterling, the market finances the deficit and there is no risk to the currency. In the mid-1960s, however, overseas residents were reluctant to acquire more sterling securities and even reluctant to retain some of those they held. Even in the ordinary course of trade there developed tendencies to part with sterling as quickly as possible and to hold on to foreign currencies for as long as possible.[28]

Since private market forces aggravated rather than helped the position of sterling in the mid-1960s, the authorities had to seek assistance from official sources, namely the International Monetary Fund and foreign central banks. It is however no business of either IMF or foreign central banks to acquire real assets in Britain, so that such assistance had to be purely financial. For a time this seemed to succeed. The scale of the assistance was impressive. It has often been related how during one night, from the 24th to the 25th November 1964, the Bank of England secured credits of $3,000 million from other central banks.[29] Added to this, there was borrowing from IMF and there were special standby agreements for special credit from foreign central banks should the need for further credit arise. The continuing deficit in 1965, and fear of a renewed deficit in 1966, led to further borrowing. When the balance of payments deteriorated again in 1967, further financial accommodation was believed to be available only at stringent terms. By then, Britain's IMF quota had been exhausted, and this already meant British monetary and fiscal affairs had to be conducted in consultation with the Fund, while further assistance had to be arranged under special terms with overseas central banks. Any assistance they gave meant that they supplied their own or other foreign currencies in exchange for sterling bills, and the time came when they no longer wished to hold too much sterling at the old exchange rate, lest confidence in their own exchange positions be endangered. The assistance received was thus not only purely financial but essentially also of a short-term nature. Even when renewed, it could not be used to finance long-term capital projects. It was borrowing for the sole purpose of bolstering up the exchange reserves at a time of an outflow of funds.

The borrowing took place under IMF rules and under special arrangements to supplement these facilities (but not to alter the rules). IMF had been set up to provide temporary financial facilities, and no other, to countries in temporary balance of payments difficulties, so that such countries could weather such problems without resort to exchange rate variations or other protectionist measures. These arrangements often succeeded in localising individual countries' balance of payments difficulties and so avoided the competitive protection and depreciations which had added to the tragedies of the 1930s. It still managed to isolate the difficulties of sterling. Had it not been for IMF and central bank cooperation in the 1960s, these difficulties of sterling might well have led to a renaissance of economic nationalism of the 1930s variety. In this respect international monetary cooperation was a success. That it failed to maintain the value of sterling was largely because it had not been designed to meet the precise problems of sterling in the mid-1960s.

The founding fathers of IMF knew a world rent asunder by strife, and they knew that competitive depreciations and other manifestations of economic nationalism had all too often fanned the flames. They also knew of a world of widespread unemployment which was often aggravated by balance of payments difficulties. Their solution for temporary balance of payments difficulties was to provide financial accommodation. This would finance such deficits when markets failed to do so. It would increase the money supply in a deficit country and so increase its participation in world economic activity. It would increase the deficit country's *absolute* advantage. The monetary accommodation made available by IMF and/or foreign central banks would then be an alternative to the increase in money supply which otherwise would have to be engineered through depreciation or devaluation. All this assumes that the deficit country has unemployed resources.

Britain had no such spare resources in 1964. Purely financial accommodation helped to maintain or increase money supply, but this was not what was really needed. What was needed was an addition to the country's real capital stock, and if foreign assistance was required this should have taken the form of a development loan. This could have been used to purchase equipment for modernisation and so could have compensated for the long years of underinvestment since the 1949 devaluation. Purely financial assistance was at best a palliative. In so far as it eased the authorities' worries about domestic money supply, it may even have been aggravating. For it deferred the need to consider domestic monetary reform and, as far as that goes, it made devaluation more rather than less certain.

If fixed exchange rates are to be maintained in times of full employment, a balance of payments deficit must be financed by an import of real capital and not just money capital. Only such loans are of lasting help which can be spent on real capital. When the market provides the appropriate capital movements, as it appears to have done in 1960, official finance is unnecessary. When the market fails to do this, official finance should do what the market fails to do. In general, in times of unemployment and balance of payments deficit, an inflow of money capital may suffice to maintain the value of the currency. In times of full employment and balance of payments deficit, only an inflow of real capital can ensure this. Such an inflow of real capital was not forthcoming in the mid-1960s. The borrowing did not facilitate more production. It only provided more money.

The IMF system just was not designed to deal with the sort of problems which faced sterling in the mid-1960s. The fault, if it was a fault, was not that the system was inherently wrong but that it did not go far enough. The quotas were too small to meet requirements and had to be supplemented by additional facilities provided by the major central banks. The IMF procedure can be cumbersome, while central banks seem to be able to lend to each other at very short notice. But most important was the fact that IMF was intended to provide purely financial accommodation and was given no power to do anything else.

None of this implies that the solution for the problems of sterling should depend solely on international action. The events of the 1960s have led to much rethinking of monetary issues and, in the years from 1968 to 1971, led to reform of monetary management in Britain. It remains to be seen whether this will strengthen sterling sufficiently that it can withstand the vagaries of the external trading position, either without deficits or with deficits which are largely financed by the market. If the market does not do so and official borrowing is to restore confidence, a development loan is more suitable than borrowing of financial paper titles to money. As it was, in and after 1964 there was purely financial borrowing and then more borrowing to repay the borrowing, none of which added to the real resources of the economy. It only added to the obligations to be met by the economy.

Perhaps this would not have mattered too much, had there not been a steady increase in the claims on the economy which arose from the government's overseas commitments. These were determined on political grounds, and it is not an economist's task to comment upon the role governments should or should not play abroad. It is legitimate however to point to the balance of payments effects of some of the decisions to increase government spending abroad. For instance, as ex-colonies became independent and ex-enemies allies, the cost of defraying expenditure on British forces in their territories was transferred from their budgets to the British budget and, in consequence, went through the exchanges. At the same time, government economic aid to overseas countries increased. Some of this aid may have benefited British exporters,[30] but since they were paid by the British government, this did not increase the country's foreign exchange earnings. Whatever the details, government expenditure overseas, which had been scaled down to a net figure between £50 and £60 million a year for the first two years after the Korean War, rose steadily thereafter. It exceeded £100 million by 1954, £200 million by 1958, £300 million by 1961 and £400 million by 1963. It reached a peak with £470 million in 1966. Then it was stabilised at around this figure for the next three years only to rise above £500 million in 1971.[31]

Whatever the proper role of British governments may be overseas, the question arises how much the government can spend overseas without inflicting at least some damage to the balance of payments. Generally, what an economy can economically afford to do beyond its borders is indicated by the balance of payments on current account. This shows by how far the country's earnings from exports exceed the country's expenditure on imports. The difference can be used to augment the exchange reserves which enables the country to spend more in future; or it can be used to finance investment overseas which means that the country acquires overseas assets and derives a future income from those assets; or it can be used by the government for its political purposes. No harm is done to the exchange reserves, as long as the augmentation of the exchange reserves, overseas investment and government expenditure overseas added together, do not exceed the balance of payments surplus on current account. But it is no small order to want an external surplus to finance a more than ninefold increase in government overseas expenditure within only fifteen years.

The *commercial* balance of payments on current account fared much better. This is the balance of payments on current account minus any net government transactions overseas. This has not been in deficit since 1955. Even in that year, the deficit was slight (£17 million). Although it is true that the commercial balance of payments on current account weakened in 1960, 1964 and 1967, it stayed in surplus of £27 million, £50 million and £148 million respectively.[32] While the balance of payments deficit in those three years coincided with a weakening of the commercial balance, it remains true to say that there would have been no deficits in the absence of rising government commitments overseas. The average commercial balance of payments on current account in 1960 to 1966 was a surplus of £337 million ranging from £27 million (1960) to £554 million (1966). The commercial balance is not the same from year to year but increases in government commitment overseas can be fairly regular burdens on the balance. In short, there was no 'chronic' *commercial* balance of payments crisis. There were political problems resulting from the winding-up of empire which cannot recur, and there was a growing sense of obligation towards poor nations which may increase. Those problems contributed to the financial difficulties which were 'solved' by means of machinery set up to meet purely commercial balance of payments problems of underemployed economies. But in the case of Britain, in 1964 to 1967, the cause of the balance of payments difficulties of the time was at least as much political as commercial, and the British economy was

6

not underemployed. Seen this way, the penalty of devaluation of the currency did not fit the 'crime'. Perhaps the economy should have been able to meet these additional obligations. Whatever should have been, the economy was charged with more and more political bills which it found increasingly difficult to meet.

When devaluation came, it was accompanied by a series of measures designed to restrict the home economy, which were thought could improve external performance. Such measures were nothing new. Each time there were balance of payments difficulties in the 1960s and earlier, the authorities tried to deal with the situation in a 'package' consisting of a variety of monetary, fiscal and physical measures of control. They varied in detail and intensity, so that it is difficult to say exactly what combination of these various methods have proved most successful in the past. In 1967, they included a rise in Bank rate from 6½ per cent to 8 per cent, which was a rise from a high rate to the highest post-war rate. Bank credit was frozen at the level then prevailing except for priority borrowers, chiefly exporters. There was also some stiffer taxation. All this was accompanied by further borrowing from abroad where the IMF gave a standby credit and so did various foreign central banks.[33]

The 'package' of 1967 was not exactly the same as that on earlier occasions. In April 1960, the authorities were worried about rising home consumption and a deterioration in the balance of payments. They dealt with the situation first by an increase in Bank rate from 4 to 5 per cent, and then with budgetary re-allocation of expenditure from consumption and in favour of industrial demand. Hire purchase controls were introduced. Later, in the same month, the Bank of England made its first calls for Special Deposits from the clearing banks—which obliged those banks to deposit part of their cash with the Bank of England. This made those banks less free to increase advances. The April 1960 measures appeared to have had some effect by the end of the year, and the balance of payments out-turn for the first quarter of 1961 was better than that for the first quarter of 1960. The same applied to all subsequent quarters of 1961. But an actual current account surplus did not emerge until the third quarter of 1961. The balance of payments improvement thus took about nine months to materialise, if the criterion is an improvement in the current balance over the corresponding quarter in the preceding year; and fifteen months if the criterion is the emergence of an actual surplus.[34]

In November 1964, the package took the form of an increase in Bank rate from 5 to 7 per cent, a surcharge on imports and a rebate granted on domestic duties paid on certain exports. There were some increases in taxation and there were substantial overseas borrowings. The balance of payments, which had in any case been improving from the third to the fourth quarter, improved further and this led to exact external balance in the first quarter of 1965. If government transactions are excluded, a surplus was attained by that time. The overall balance of payments on current account went into surplus in the fourth quarter of 1965. Thus, in so far as the November 1964 measures influenced the balance of payments out-turn, the time during which they became effective was somewhere between one quarter and one year.[35]

In July 1966, there were renewed worries about the state of the economy and the fear of a return of balance of payments deficits. Taxes were sharply increased, building restrictions were imposed, there was a cut in government expenditure and a cut in the travel allowance overseas. Other exchange control measures too were intensified. There was a complete standstill on wages and salaries for six months, to be followed by severe restraint for another six months. The balance of payments, which had been running in deficit during the first three quarters of the year, turned into surplus by the fourth quarter. That quarter also showed a considerable improvement over the corresponding quarter in 1965.[36] Now it is never possible to say that, because the balance of payments improved after such and such measures had been taken, those measures were the sole or even the direct cause of the improvement. Nevertheless, if it is believed that the authorities' actions were effective, the July 1966 measures were effective within less than six months.

Thus, from 1960 to 1966, increasingly severe measures were taken to protect the balance of payments. If these measures can be credited with the subsequent improvement, they worked with increasing rapidity.

The package which accompanied the 1967 devaluation, was probably the most severe of any of the package measures taken in the 1960s. Bank rate reached the highest level since 1914 and the highest in peacetime during the present century. Credit was not only restrained but frozen for all private borrowers other than exporters. Tax concessions for employers of labour in manufacturing industry, only recently introduced in the form of a selective employment tax premium, were abolished. If any package was severe and should have worked quickly, it was that which accompanied the 1967 devaluation. But, this time, the balance of payments turn-round was rather slow in coming. In the first three quarters of 1968, there were worse balance of payments out-turns than in the corresponding quarters of 1967. The fourth quarter, though still in deficit, showed some improvement over the last quarter of 1967. But the balance of payments result for the last quarter of 1967 had been exceptionally bad, not least because devaluation was widely anticipated. (This meant at first that imports were hurried in. Later, when devaluation actually came about half-way through that quarter, some importers were caught and had to pay more in sterling. Exports were delayed, sometimes until after the end of the year. There also was a dock strike.) It may be more useful to compare the last quarter of 1968 with the last quarter of 1966. If so, the fourth quarter of 1968 was disappointing. In fact, it was one of the worst out-turns for the fourth quarter in any year in the 1960s. There was no balance of payments surplus until the first quarter of 1969, and there was no substantial balance of payments surplus until the third quarter of 1969.[37] By then, however, other measures had been taken, especially in November 1968.

Thus, the 'package' which included devaluation worked more slowly than earlier packages which had not. The 1960 measures attempted to defer consumption, while the measures of 1964, 1966 and 1967 (excluding devaluation itself) were attempts to cut consumption. In so far as these measures succeeded, they succeeded in reducing sterling claims on resources and so had the effects of a cut in money supply. Now, one lesson of this century's history is that the balance of payments almost invariably responds fairly quickly to changes in money supply. This was so in the days of straightforward monetary credit control in the 1900s to 1914 and in the 1920s. It was also true in the 1950s and 1960s, when control was exercised in more roundabout ways, and it became quite clear again with the strengthening of monetary controls from November 1968 onwards. Devaluation, however, increases money supply.

The effects were immediate. There was a 'long Christmas' from devaluation day in November 1967, to budget day in March 1968. Although assured from the highest authority that the pound in his pocket was not devalued, the man-in-the-street seemed to do everything he could to get that pound out of his pocket. He became a man-in-the-shops. This mopped up quite a few potential exports.

There was no change until the 1968 budget, when an un-precedently large increase in indirect taxation was planned to take £900 million out of consumers' pockets. Although this resulted in a slump in the consumer durables market, overall this arrested rather than reversed the trend in consumer spending. Another dose was applied in the 1969 budget, and again the effect was stabilisation rather than overall reduction in consumers' expenditure.[38]

The 'sale' was at home where devaluation was adding to money supply, rather than abroad where it did not. Of course this does not mean to say that consumers had been handed extra money on devaluation day. But they sensed that 'every-thing would go up' in price at a time when the money supply was destined to rise at a substantially faster rate than the supply of goods could conceivably increase. This was at least one of the reasons why devaluation led to an increase in imports. Had this just been a rise in the value of imports, that would have been an expected result of devaluation which raised sterling prices of overseas goods. But imports rose by volume as well as by value and, what is more, rose by volume at a faster rate than before devaluation.

There was a time when it was reasonable to expect no such consequences from a lowering of the exchange rate. Thus, in 1931 and to a lesser extent even in 1949, the British market for primary products was so predominant that overseas suppliers adjusted their prices to British prices in order to maintain the volume of their sales as far as they could. By 1967, the majority of overseas suppliers did not consider the British market so overwhelmingly important and charged British importers as much as they otherwise would have done in terms of their own currencies. It is more difficult to evaluate whether there has been a similar change in respect of imported manufactures. For, in 1931, imported manufactures were penalised by new tariffs and,

in 1949, imports were controlled by foreign exchange alloca-
tions. Moreover, neither in 1931 nor in 1949 were manufactures
as important in total imports as they were to become in the
course of the 1960s. What guidance twentieth-century history
provides is that imported manufactures tend to sell in Britain
at prices not far from those of similar home produced goods,
subject only to quality differentials.[39] They did not have to cut
their prices but could wait, often not too long, for British
prices to catch up with theirs.

This still does not explain the rise of the volume of imports in
1968, which was most marked in manufactures.[40] Again,
foreign suppliers did not have to do anything. By now it is
known that the increased sterling earnings of exporters led to
an increase in money supply. In part this was due to higher
export earnings and in part to multiplier effects of exporters'
increased spending; and there were other forces at work as well.
Whatever the cause, the increase in money supply came to
approximately 10 per cent.[41] This additional money became
available in an economy where the authorities sought to
restrict demand rather than increase supply of domestically
produced goods. Since the economy was already fully employed and there were no additional domestic supplies, the
increase in purchasing power available led to a spillover of
British demand into overseas markets. Amongst the beneficiaries of the British 1967 devaluation must then be counted a
number of overseas suppliers and especially suppliers of manufactures. Only in the case of food, was there some response to
higher import prices. Even in this case, the volume of imports
rose in 1968 over the volume of 1967. But this was a mere
3 per cent, against a rise of 11 per cent for all imports and
17 per cent for manufactures.[42] Moreover food imports subsequently fell back while other imports did not. Both volumes
and values of non-food imports continued to rise, with

volumes rising more than values especially in manufactures.

The same happened to exports in 1968 and 1969, and again this was most marked in manufactures. But in the case of exports the 'sale' was soon over. The position was reversed in 1970 and 1971, when export prices rose by more than export volumes. Yet 1970 and 1971 were the years of Britain's greatest balance of payments success to date.

Interpretation of such information is always fraught with difficulties. These are all the greater in the case of the 1967 devaluation because monetary measures taken in November 1968 and after, exerted an at least equally powerful influence. Perhaps it is best to concentrate on what happened to volumes of exports in 1968, which at least is a post-devaluation year before the monetary reforms.

In 1968, the volume of both total exports and exports of manufactures rose by 14 per cent. This was by more than the increase in the volume of all imports (11 per cent) but by less than the increase in imports of manufactures (17 per cent). This suggests that in the exchange of manufactures for primary products, devaluation was followed by an improvement in Britain's performance. But in the exchange of manufactures for manufactures, this was not the case.

In the exchange of manufactures for primary products, price considerations are usually overriding. Exporters of the various manufactured products from Britain compete with exporters from other industrial countries for the market. If British exporters can sell cheap because, after devaluation, they produce cheap, they can snatch a competitive advantage over their rivals. While this is not altogether impossible in the exchange of manufactures for manufactures, this does not seem to happen to any great extent. Exporters of manufactures do not often go in for competitive price wars with established rivals in the various industrial importing countries. Just as much as foreign suppliers of manufactures to Britain normally do best by pricing in relation to the nearest British-made substitutes and concentrate on quality, so British exporters will normally act likewise when they export to countries with established manufacturing industries. Now devaluation encourages home producers to concentrate on quantity rather than on quality. This helps British exports of manufactures relative to overseas suppliers of non-manufactures. It does not help the export of British manufactures relative to overseas suppliers of manufactures. The encouragement to export more rather than to export better may actually be a handicap in the commercial relations with manufacturing interests abroad. The quantitative results for British exports relative to British imports in 1968 bear this out.

So does the remarkable growth of the volume of imported manufactures, with volumes rising more than values. This is not necessarily an indication of improved competitive performance of overseas suppliers. Rather it means that, in a country where production is encouraged to be as cheap as possible, lower and lower quality foreign goods become acceptable.

These results showed most clearly in 1968 but have continued during the following years. Only in 1969, when money supply was held constant, did the volume of British exports rise by more than the volume of imports of manufactures.

Exporters knew this or at least acted as if they knew. To sell cheap to the world's most rapidly growing markets, which were also the world's wealthiest industrial markets, was futile. The goods could not be sold entirely out of line with the prices prevailing in those markets in terms of the currencies of the importing countries, so that at least some of the 'benefit' of devaluation went to overseas importing agencies. There was no point in engaging in price wars. Often this would have led to trouble with agents who were also agents for suppliers from elsewhere. Always it would have meant that for any 10 per cent cut in the foreign currency price, the British exporter would have had to sell 11 per cent more in quantity just to break even. This was quite impractical. Moreover, the rise in domestic factor prices made it impossible to hold sterling prices.

If factor prices tend to rise to offset devaluation in times of high employment, so do product prices. Even in 1968, when export prices in sterling did not rise as much as export volumes, export prices of British manufactures rose by 9 per cent, and in 1968 and 1969 taken together by 12 per cent. By the end of 1971, they had risen by almost one-third over the pre-devaluation level.[43] But this was not enough to fit the $2·40 exchange rate. It has been shown before how devaluation unleashed tendencies for British wages to rise in a direction of about 16·7 per cent above American wages, at any rate for as long as Britain maintained a high level of employment. It has also been shown that, in so far as 16·7 per cent is a guide, this was attained towards the end of 1971. The 16·7 per cent is only a guide to the extent to which British wages were to rise more than American wages after devaluation. Similarly, 16·7 per cent is only a guide to the extent to which British export prices in sterling were likely to be driven above American export prices. If all export prices are taken into consideration, then British export prices rose by 6 per cent more than American prices in 1968 and maintained this position in 1969. In 1970 the rise in British export prices since 1967 came to 7 per cent above the rise in American export prices, and in 1971 this excess rise came to 13 per cent. An excess rise of 16·7 per cent appears to have been attained by May 1972.[44] By that time, however, the dollar had fallen relative to sterling.

This is at best a rough indication of the relative price movements which followed devaluation. Very roughly, it indicates that British export prices in sterling had risen by sufficiently more than American export prices in dollars, so as to offset the 1967 devaluation approximately four years later. Currencies are neutral between commodities so that the overall picture is relevant, although the commodity composition of the two countries' export trades differs.

If the question is what happened to price-competition between the two countries and the industrial world as a whole, it is best to look at exports of manufactures alone, since British exports are largely manufactures, and at dollar prices. Dollar prices of British exports fell initially, but by 1971 they had caught up. They had risen by slightly over 16 per cent over the 1967 level, as compared with a $15\frac{1}{2}$ per cent price rise in American exports of manufactures and a 16 per cent rise in all industrial countries' exports of manufactures.[45] Seen this way, British dollar prices moved in line with world prices. The sharper rise in sterling prices was an adjustment to world prices.

If export prices, in sterling, adjusted themselves towards the 1967 exchange rate, this does not mean to say that they were 'right' in 1967. As in the case of wages, they may have been too high or too low in 1967. In this connection, it may be worth recalling that Britain's best balance of payments performance was in 1970 and 1971, and that this depended more on rising export prices than on rising export volumes. On this ground alone, it would seem that prices had been too low in relation to the exchange rate.

Once export prices were rising, the same was likely to happen to domestic prices. Few firms can afford to sell cheaper at home than in export markets. In any case, if they did they would soon cause resentment in overseas markets which do not like to be discriminated against. Export prices and home prices are then likely to move in the same direction.

Today's worker and today's trader find ways of defending themselves against having their worth reduced, even if the poor cannot. But until today's worker and today's trader have succeeded, the economy stands still or almost still. It is misdirected into purely quantitative growth on the basis of cheap labour, and if it cannot have cheap labour it cannot grow this way. Qualitative growth is less necessary as long as labour is cheap, and there are not enough funds to pay for it when labour will not stay cheap. The outside world is asked to take more cheap goods but it also sends more, so that the balance of payments does best when export prices rise to be once more in line with world prices at the new exchange rate. When the equilibrating price movements have worked through the system, the economy can move again. But it has stood still, while the outside world has not. In consequence it offers a more antiquated assortment of goods than its industrial rivals. Since the Third World too does not want those goods, there are renewed balance of payments worries. These points apply in times of high employment and growing world trade. By contrast, in times of deepening depression, it would be all to the good to delay change and stand still. That is why these points do not apply to the 1920s and 1930s. But they apply to the 1950s and 1960s.

All this happened after 1949 and eventually led to 1967. All this happened in 1967 and even more quickly led . . .

No. None of this is inevitable. But once a devaluation has led to the predictable equilibrating factor and product price movements and these have worked through the system, the economy can resume qualitative growth only at a handicap There are three choices. One is to devalue again and repeat past woes, more quickly each time as experience is gained of what is likely to happen. The second is to seek a foreign loan to speed up development and overcome the handicap. The third is for the authorities to tighten monetary controls in ways that fit the age. This was the path chosen in 1968–71. Following November 1968 the balance of payments improved, but there also followed a rise in unemployment. The problem of where to draw the line between the currency's efficiency and employment functions remained unresolved.

Chapter Three   CREDIT
CONTROL
1900-1971

The balance of payments went into surplus in 1969, and record surpluses were achieved for three years running. This was after devaluation but rather a long time afterwards. As shown before, each of the 'package' measures taken earlier in the 1960s was soon followed by improvements in the balance of payments. Only after the comparatively mild package of April 1960 did this take more than a year, while about three months sufficed after July 1966. The devaluation of November 1967 and the accompanying package were not followed by a quick improvement in the balance of payments. The balance of payments for 1968 as a whole was slightly worse than that for 1967 as a whole. On a quarterly basis, there were worse balance of payments results in the first three quarters of 1968 than the corresponding quarters of 1967. In the fourth quarter of 1968, the deficit was less than in the fourth quarter of 1967 but the latter had been influenced by acceleration of imports and delays in exports because devaluation was widely expected. Quarterly balance of payments statistics are available from 1958 onwards,[1] and the fourth quarter figures were worse than in 1968 only in 1964 and 1967. There was a small surplus in the first quarter of 1969, but this was still less than the surplus of the first quarter of 1967. A substantial surplus did not emerge until the second half of 1969. By that time a number of other measures had been taken. The mere fact that more and more controls seemed necessary 'to make devaluation work' indicates that the authorities were dissatisfied with the way it worked.

95

Amongst those measures was the increase in indirect taxation in the 1968 budget to stop the 'long Christmas', and the renewed doses of the same medicine in the 1969 budget. These were attempts to make consumers do with fewer goods, as if they had saved more of their money[2] (though the 'savings' went to the Exchequer). There were also attempts to make them do with different goods. To this end different tax rates were applied to different commodities, in order to lead to 'expenditure-switching' away from imports and any home-produced goods for which there might be an export market.[3]

In retrospect it seems that, while these tax increases may have helped to stop the rise in consumer expenditure, real incomes had been devalued so that there was not too much to stop.[4] Consumers knew that their money would become worth less and tried to get goods while they could. They also knew when budget day was coming and that governments were prone to raise domestic taxation whenever there were external payments problems. Hence they anticipated both. Nor was there too much to 'switch'. Apart from the difficulties in estimating accurately what sort of tax change would be required for each commodity, to lead to whatever switching was thought desirable, devaluation itself had produced a different kind of 'switch'. As shown in the previous chapter, it led to a 'sale' of British goods abroad *and* of foreign goods in Britain. More of yesterday's goods were offered abroad and lower quality home or foreign goods became acceptable at home. Of course, lower quality does not necessarily mean that 1968 standards were absolutely lower than 1967 standards. What it means is that 1968 standards were not as much above 1967 standards as would normally be expected in a growth economy. Since the outside world was not so easily content, it just meant lower quality to and from Britain than to and from the industrial world as a whole.

This is another way of saying that devaluation had raised the British 1967 economy's absolute advantage, with the result that more goods produced in 1967 ways could be exported and imported in 1968. Since 1968 goods could not vary too much from 1967 goods, this may not have mattered much in the short run. Generally such delay in change becomes apparent only after some years have passed; and how many years that is, depends on the circumstances of each trade. Whatever the details, technological opportunities for change come sooner and goods date earlier in the modern industrial world than previously this century. If these opportunities are not taken, because the need for innovation is obscured, the quality of goods offered at home or abroad does not improve as much as possible. Yet in the days of intra-industry specialisation, the road to greater comparative advantage is through innovation. The switch which was effected was a switch in demand towards 1967 goods rather than 1968 goods, just as much as the switch in production was one to prolong the life of 1967 methods.

Some of the other measures taken at the time supported those devaluation effects. Once the increase in taxation had stopped the long Christmas, it made goods less saleable in the home market. Whatever else this did, it cannot have been conducive towards innovative activity. Nor could any other measures which made goods less saleable.

Most notable amongst those other measures were the attempts at formulating a policy for personal incomes. The idea was not new. It had been attempted as 'wage restraint' in the late 1940s and as 'pay pause' in the early 1960s. On both occasions wage restraint was sought through suasion. In 1966, it was named 'incomes policy' and based on statutory power. Initially it was proclaimed as part of the policy to avoid devaluation, though after devaluation it was said to be a way of making devaluation work.

7

This is not the place to deal with the intricacies of the con-
troversial issue of whether such a policy is economically
desirable. Let it suffice to say that it was a policy of postponing
price and wage changes until the specially created National
Board for Prices and Incomes had pronounced on the merits
of the case. This had to take account of the national interest,
which effectively meant the Government-declared norm for
such increases which varied from nil to rates considered com-
mensurate with the rise in productivity. Sympathetic commentators credited the policy with having kept down the rate
of increase of weekly wage rates by about 1 per cent in 1966
and between 1¼ and 1½ per cent in 1967 but were non-committal
about the effects on earnings.[5] This may have accounted for a
fall in the share of wages in national income from 40 per cent
in 1965 and 1966 to about 39 per cent in 1967 and 1968,[6] but
this result is also compatible with a general slowing down of the
economy which reduces the demand for current toil.

The policy was successful in as far as it had the same results
as the increase in indirect taxation, since it also lowered the
prospects for selling goods in the home market. It tried to do
so by keeping factor prices down. Again, this was not conducive to innovation. The reason is that any policy which keeps
factor prices down reduces the need to innovate. Since the
policy also tried to freeze relative factor prices, it discouraged
change of employment from less lucrative activities to more
lucrative ones. This again discouraged change.[7]

The personal incomes policy, like fiscal policy and eventually
devaluation, was an attempt to stabilise the market without
resort to an effective monetary policy. Supporters of a personal
incomes policy often readily admit that the market could be
disciplined more effectively by holding money supply constant.
Their fear is that this would lead to widespread unemployment.[8]

Their view seemed to get confirmation in 1969. In that year, money supply was held constant,[9] unemployment rose and there was not even price stability. A policy of immiseration without gain cannot commend itself, but it is a policy of immiseration only if carried to excess. There were special pressures to keep the rate of increase of money supply down in 1969, and the authorities overshot the mark. Even the most convinced monetarists do not want to keep money supply constant. They tend to argue in favour of a steady and controlled increase in money supply[10] as opposed to the rather passive monetary policy of pre-1968 days. But this is going ahead of the narrative.

For good reasons or bad, monetary policy was still in disfavour in 1967 and in the early months of 1968, at least as far as control of the domestic economic situation was concerned. Devaluation was thought of as a price policy which had moved prices of British goods in favour of foreign consumers and prices of foreign goods against British consumers, and it had also lowered the price of British labour relative to the price of foreign labour. This was to be supported by policies which were also designed to work on prices. The fiscal measures mentioned earlier were meant to move prices further against British consumers, and the personal incomes policy was meant to keep factor prices down. There was to be no equilibrating rise in factor prices after devaluation and there was to be a perpetual 'sale' of British goods. Devaluation leads to such a 'sale' through quantitative expansion. Since there was little or no room for quantitative expansion in a fully employed economy, the supporting measures were meant to stem any tendencies towards quantitative expansion by making goods less saleable in the home market.

Neither devaluation nor those supporting measures encouraged qualitative growth. Devaluation encouraged quantitative growth and the supporting measures stopped that as far as possible. There was still a 'sale' of yesteryear's goods *from* Britain. There was also one *in* Britain. The reason was that money supply had increased after devaluation and the additional money was spent. It could be spent on British goods, but this added to pressure on resources and drove up prices. It could also be spent on foreign goods, where the additional pressures created by British demand could have only slight effects on resources and prices.

The situation in 1968 illustrated how devaluation raises an economy's absolute advantage in participation in world economic activity without structural change at home. Since this led to an increased *volume* of imports as well as of exports, there was no relief for the balance of payments. Generally such relief will be the less, the greater the volume of imports relative to exports—and had there been no excess of imports over exports, devaluation would not have been contemplated in 1967.

The authorities were still faced with two major problems. One was how to stem the flow of imports. The other was how to control the rise in *aggregate* money incomes without risk of unemployment. Imports will be considered first.

If devaluation was widely thought of as a policy which works on price relationships rather than on aggregate incomes, and if the fiscal and personal incomes policies to support it worked on product and factor prices, the question arises whether a more severe price policy could not have been applied to imports. Was this not the missing link to make price policies successful in bringing about the desired improvement in the balance of payments?

To some extent, imports were subjected to price policy since they were not exempt from the increase in indirect taxation. In this respect at least, there was no new discrimination between imports and home produced goods. If the authorities were right not to discriminate against imports at a time of excess imports, they must have viewed the problem as one of general excess spending in this country compared with spending elsewhere. This is a problem of money supply rather than one of prices of individual products and factors. Nevertheless, given all the interventions with prices of individual products and factors at the time, and given that imports were running too high for external balance, the question remains why special price policies were not attempted in relation to imports.

Part of the answer is that devaluation itself had already raised prices of imports in terms of sterling so that no further action may have been thought necessary. Another part of the answer is that the only other price policy with a direct impact on imports would have been an increase in the tariff. This is one of the oldest known remedies for excess imports. It had been tried as recently as 1964, when the package of that year included a temporary surcharge on imports of manufactures. But this had been in contravention of several international trade agreements and greeted with such an outcry that a repetition of the same policy only three years later would almost certainly have led to retaliation. The whole edifice of international tariff agreements would have been at risk, and the latest of these agreements had been concluded only a few months earlier.[11] Such action could have been contemplated only if the authorities had wished for a British withdrawal from world trade.

There are times when such a withdrawal can be advocated, at least from a purely national point of view. What is involved may be seen most clearly with the help of a flashback to 1931. Then, the depreciation of sterling was accompanied by a return to general protection. Both in 1931 and in 1967, pressure of events forced the authorities to abandon the formerly prevailing exchange rate. On both occasions this involved changes in

credit policy and the changes in credit policy had implications
for import policy. In 1931, the then known monetary controls
were relaxed or abandoned as unworkable. Credit was allowed
to expand and interest rate policy suspended. In consequence
the authorities had to rely increasingly on direct controls of
the working of the economy. But such direct controls might
have been frustrated by external free trade. Free trade was
abandoned.

A lowering of the exchange rate and an increase in tariffs are
sometimes thought to be alternative ways of correcting a
balance of payments deficit.[12] There may be situations where
they are. In retrospect, it seems probable that this was not so in
1931. Whether driven by logic, or just by instinctive reaction
to the pressure of events, the authorities chose two policies
which were compatible in the circumstances of their time.
Once depreciation had allowed for credit expansion, there was
more money. Additional money can be spent on home produced goods but can also be spent on imports. If the depreciation was to lead to a 'sale', this could have been a 'sale' of
domestic or imported goods. Had the major trading countries
acted in concert, the way they have learnt to behave in the
post-war world, it would not have mattered too much where
the 'sale' was and whence the goods came. In the circumstances
of 1931, such cooperation was unheard of. Since other countries
too suffered from industrial depression and took independent
action to deal with the situation, the prospects for exports were
limited. The 'sale' had to be in the home market. This market
was to be protected in order to ensure that the 'sale' would
relieve unemployment at home rather than abroad.[13]

At first sight the logic of the price policies of 1967–8 points
the same way. Devaluation and the personal incomes policy
worked in the direction of lowering domestic factor prices
while devaluation and increased indirect taxation raised product

prices. To close the circle of controls, other than credit control, there might have been a case for higher import duties in order to ensure that the 'sale' would be one of home produced goods only. In fact this could not have worked in 1967. The increase in money supply which follows devaluation can fill empty work benches only where there are empty work benches. If there are none or only few, the expansion of the economy depends largely on more specialisation between the home economy and the rest of the world. A withdrawal from world trade is then inimical to the country's long-term interests and would be of little or no help even in the short run.

Increased Government intervention in the details of prices does, however, imply a withdrawal from world values. In the absence of other policies, increased protection would seem almost inevitable. The case is re-enforced if a devaluation raises the country's absolute advantage and, therefore, yesteryear's imports as well as yesteryear's exports, as happened in 1968. Some way had to be found to deal with excess imports.

In the 1930s, credit control could be relaxed because increased employment mattered more than increased efficiency. In the 1960s, the opposite applied. This is more easily said than done, not only because monetary policy was still widely viewed with suspicion, but also because most of the known monetary controls had been evolved in different circumstances and did not quite fit the requirements of the late 1960s. This will be the subject of later sections. Here let it suffice to say that the unexpected behaviour of the *volume* of imports, after devaluation in 1967, revealed the difficulties of intervention through prices without special intervention in import prices. The logic of the 1930s was lacking. For whatever else one may think of the policies of the 1930s, there was consistency between depreciation and credit expansion with the return to protection and increasingly detailed direct Government intervention in prices and production. There was no such consistency in 1967 and to November 1968. Devaluation was accompanied by a package which included the then known methods of credit restraint, such as a freeze of clearing bank advances and a higher Bank rate; and since there was no faith that such a combination of policies could work, this was supplemented by the price policies discussed above. Intensified direct interventions with prices were, however, inconsistent with the greater freeing of external trade agreed to on conclusion of the Kennedy Round earlier in 1967. These inconsistencies became apparent when imports would not respond. It was the 'misbehaviour' of imports which ultimately led to the search for more effective credit policies.

Generally, what happens to the relative volume of credit or, to use fashionable parlance, money supply, determines relative spending here and abroad. There is no known precise relationship: in different countries, with different banking systems and different savings habits and different industrial structures, the response to any given percentage increase in money supply cannot be the same. All that can be said is that a country's money supply has expanded too much if it overspends more than other countries do. In this context, overspending means that domestic goods and factors can be obtained only at rising prices, and this leads to rising attractiveness of imports. In the 1960s, all industrial countries went in for some overspending and, therefore, experienced domestic inflation, but some did so more than others. Those who went too far were faced with balance of payments difficulties. Seen this way, the balance of payments is a monetary phenomenon, curable only by monetary means—though one may add: provided there are known monetary means which fit the real situation.

This is not news. It has been known for a long time. In Britain, in the 1950s and 1960s where action against inflation was taken only when the authorities got worried lest an adverse balance of payments undermine the exchange value of sterling, the various package measures always included some monetary measures. These were often crude and negative, such as limitations on the advances clearing banks could make to their customers, and they were often intended to affect the external situation more than the domestic one, such as interest rate changes which were alleviated by tax allowances for anyone within the country who made interest payments. Moreover, it was always realised that price policy would eventually affect aggregate incomes, and that changes in money supply would eventually affect prices.

There was sometimes a deliberate choice of policy according to whether the impact on prices was considered more urgent than the impact on money incomes, and vice versa. Sometimes however the choice was more limited simply because the appropriate monetary policies had not yet been worked out.

An example is the fact that domestic and imported goods were identically treated in the 1968 and 1969 tax increases. This suggests that the problem of excess imports was seen as a problem of there being too much money about for spending. Although the attack came via prices, the increased tax content of prices would transfer money from the general public to the Exchequer. Eventually this would reduce the amount of money available for the private purchase of goods. 'Eventually' however meant 'by the time the money supply was restricted' and this did not come about in 1968. While it did not, the attack on imports via prices showed no results. Either there had to be a special price increase for imports, which was ruled out, or there was need for a direct attack on overspending which meant restraint in the growth of money supply.

The continuing rise in the volume of imports led to rethinking and eventually to the monetary reform of 1971. It came in response to the ineffectiveness of other measures to secure balance of payments results as quickly as desired. Whatever the merits of increased price interventions in different circumstances and for other purposes, as aids to the solution of a balance of payments problem at a time of high employment and growth of world trade, they are at best stop-gap measures.

So were the first post-devaluation essays in monetary control. These included more external borrowing which entitled the International Monetary Fund to be consulted on British monetary and fiscal affairs. Perhaps this contributed to the reshaping of ideas, but it did not give the authorities immediate control over the situation. There was a rise in Bank rate, which was more intended to attract financial funds to London or to stay in London, rather than to have a major impact on the domestic situation. In so far as this succeeded, it reduced the need for tighter control of the supply of sterling. Nevertheless, tighter monetary control was attempted through the renewed freezing of bank advances, but this applied only to the London clearing banks and Scottish banks. Even where it applied, it did not necessarily restrict credit to the same extent, since at any one point of time not all overdraft facilities are drawn upon to the limit. Effectively, this made it more difficult to get new overdraft facilities, but it will never be known how far established borrowers were really inconvenienced. The only way to ensure at least some cutback in previously arranged borrowing facilities seemed to be an actual reduction in bank advances rather than a mere freeze. This was attempted in two stages. In May 1968 the banks were ordered to keep the volume of advances to private borrowers at the level then prevailing, which was about 4 per cent above that of November 1967. Previously exporters had been exempt from the ceiling and this accounted for much of the rise in advances. Henceforth, exporters were still to be given priority but within the total ceiling. This meant a quantitative cutback at least for some non-exporters. The next step was taken in November 1968 when the authorities ordered a cutback of total advances to the private sector to 98 per cent of the November 1967 level. This was a sharp cut, since bank advances (excluding advances to nationalised industries) were then 6 per cent higher than a year earlier.[14] Later on, in the budget of 1969, tax relief on most kinds of personal borrowing was withdrawn. This made borrowing more expensive and so re-enforced the November 1968 measures which had made it quantitatively more difficult.

Although in the event bank advances were not cut back to the extent the authorities had ordered, and the result was a freeze rather than an actual reduction, the November 1968 measure marks a step in the direction of making control more equally effective for all private-sector borrowers. It also enabled the Chancellor of the Exchequer in May 1969, to reiterate to the International Monetary Fund his 'intent' to keep domestic credit expansion within a predetermined level,[15] a pledge first given in return for a stand-by credit at the time of devaluation.

While the authorities were groping towards a way of gaining effective control over money supply, the stubborn rise of imports required immediate attention.

This was given, also in November 1968, in the form of an import deposit scheme. Importers of industrial goods had to deposit half of the value of their imports with H.M. Customs for a period of six months and free of interest. This rule applied for one year. It was renewed in November 1969 for one more year though the amount of the deposit was reduced. Such a policy could be only temporary, since after the first six months repayments were made to the importers and the original effect was lost. The original effect was that funds were tied up. In consequence, the usable money supply was reduced. Since imports tend to be financed on credit, this meant a corresponding tying up of loanable funds. Imports had been unresponsive to any of the other policies which were tried, and a way was sought which would apply credit control to imports before credit control in general had become tight enough to make special treatment of imports unnecessary. When the scheme expired, the last repayments could be used to loosen the grip of the authorities on money supply at a time when unemployment was rising in 1970–1.

The import deposit scheme was internationally more acceptable than an increase in the tariff would have been. It did not contravene the letter of any trade agreement and was, by its very nature, bound to be ephemeral. It did not directly affect the prices of imports to purchasers. Its significance probably lay more in that funds were frozen than that they were frozen at the point of importation. Although there are luxury items amongst industrial imports, much of the growing import trade in manufactures consists of producer goods; and the demand for such imports is dependent on the nature and level of activity within the country. This in turn is influenced by credit control. A tightening of credit control at a time of high employment discourages the purchase of low quality goods, whether home produced or imported, but encourages the purchase of factor-saving equipment. Imports slowed down in 1969, but the rise in imports of engineering goods more than outweighed falls in textiles and other imports with a relatively lower skill content.[16] Tighter credit control thus helped to reverse the 'sale' conditions created by devaluation.

If the import deposit scheme and the quantitative control of bank advances were crude, ephemeral and imperfectly working measures of credit control, they were nonetheless more effective than what had gone before. True, in 1969, the fiscal harvest of the 1968 budget came in and this had its effect on containing the amount of money held in private hands. But money gathered by the Exchequer is spent and, if the Exchequer gets more money than it needs for current expenditure, the difference is largely used to retire National Debt. A debtor cannot burn any money he receives, lest confidence in his future creditworthiness be undermined and, as long as there is a National Debt, the Exchequer is a debtor. The authorities had no choice but to use the budget surplus to repurchase a portion of the National Debt. It so happens that amongst the principal holders of National Debt are banks and other financial institutions. Those institutions got more cash and could use it. This made it all the more important to control bank advances. The ball was back in the court of credit control.

Whatever the details, credit was kept tight after the November 1968 measures. The 'sale' was largely over. The balance of payments went into surplus, but the economy continued to stagnate and unemployment rose.

2 OLD STYLE MONETARY CONTROLS

The more effective credit control from November 1968 onwards was followed by the desired balance of payments turn-round but also by further stagnation of the economy. Bank advances are chiefly needed for the day-to-day finance of business as it is. Traditional business was already handicapped by rising labour costs, and to these difficulties were now added difficulties in getting money just to carry on. Innovating activities did not fully compensate to take up the slack. At least one of the reasons was that innovation was not so necessary in Britain as in some other countries, because the low exchange rate had made British labour costs low by international standards. While this continued, traditional activities were too discouraged and new activities were not sufficiently encouraged to maintain the level of employment. In consequence, satisfaction with the balance of payments surpluses in 1969–71 was rather muted. There was a nagging suspicion that this was being achieved while the economy was still falling behind other industrial economies and that the problems of 1967 might recur. So powerful were these fears that in June 1972 the (then higher) exchange rate could not be held, although the exchange reserves were at record levels and the balance of payments was in surplus.

The events of mid-1972 were to underline that the exchange value of sterling depends on how it performs its functions of command, and that a deterioration of the balance of payments is a symptom rather than 'the' cause of a fall in the exchange rate. If sterling is not to go on falling, confidence must be restored in the ability of the authorities to control credit. It so happened that, during the first half of 1972 the monetary system was in process of being overhauled. As will be shown below, this involved a once and for all increase in money supply. In terms of past policies this was inflationary. Such belief was strengthened by frequent assertions that the increase in money supply would facilitate growth and relieve unemployment. Markets persuaded themselves that sterling was once more getting out of control. They heard a traditional explanation, saw that all the traditional devices of monetary policy were still there and had little faith in any of them. It remains to be seen whether they were right, or whether the rearrangement of old devices, in 1971, will amount to a new and effective way of credit control.

What they had seen in the preceding years only underlined their suspicions. True, the balance of payments problem seemed solved in 1969–71, but there were domestic difficulties, and the solution of both external and domestic difficulties at one and the same time seemed as far away as ever. This was a somewhat superficial view. Devaluation and credit control had different effects on traditional and innovative activities at home. Where one helped, the other hindered. The result was that home activities stagnated. They are however the only possible sources of the exports it was intended to promote. Total imports did not respond to devaluation in the way which had been widely expected, but eventually responded to credit control. All the same, the methods of credit control of November 1968 which were finally followed by the hoped-for balance of payments turn-round, were rather makeshift. Import deposits were inherently ephemeral, while the cutback in bank advances had become an effective freeze only after much scolding and even fining of the clearing banks.[17] Although effective for a while, there could not be much faith that similar makeshifts could be successfully tried again before long. The authorities were aware of this and tried to introduce more automatic monetary controls. These were still in process of being introduced when exchange difficulties arose in June 1972.

The new controls will be considered in Chapter 4 below. Here let it be asked why the old controls had become so emaciated that they needed the crutches of quantitative controls decreed by the Chancellor. There had been a time when monetary control was thought to be a technicality, best left to the Bank and of no direct concern to the Chancellor. If the monetary system works smoothly, the Chancellor can always be content with a watching brief; and should one be found to meet the requirements of the 1970s, he will be able to sleep through International Monetary Fund meetings whenever exchange rates are discussed.

Monetary control works best when the techniques which have been evolved fit the trading requirements of the age. It can be exercised through working on interest rates or on the quantity of money. If control is through interest rates, this is control through the price of money which eventually will affect the quantity of money. If control is through the quantity of money, this will eventually affect the price of money, namely the rate of interest. The difference is the point of intervention. The policy introduced in September 1971, is intended to work on the quantity of money and to leave interest rates to find their own level in the market. Under the new approach, the Bank's lending rate is meant to follow market rates of interest rather than lead them. This is the reverse of the position at the beginning of the century, when a change in Bank rate led market rates of interest and the quantity of money was left to respond. These are the two possible extremes of credit policy. Compromise positions are possible. Thus even early this century, Bank rate policy was sometimes supported by open market operations. (This meant that, through buying and selling of long-term government securities for cash, the Bank of England affected the quantity of money in circulation more immediately than if it had waited for the change in interest rates to have that effect.) In the 1930s, when Bank rate was in abeyance, open market operations were the only possible credit policy. In the 1950s and 1960s, when Bank rate was restored as an active instrument of policy, it was not used on its own but in conjunction with fiscal controls and directives relating to the volume of bank credit.

As the trading position changed in the course of the century, so attitudes towards monetary policy changed. Perhaps this can be best illustrated by means of a short sketch of the position at the beginning of the century, when Bank rate was a powerful instrument of policy.[18] The efficacy of Bank rate can be judged according to whether the following conditions are satisfied. One is that monetary policy must fit the credit requirements of industry and trade. Another is that variations in Bank rate directly and immediately affect the price of the kind of securities which are most widely used to finance production and trade. Last and not least, comes the question whether Bank rate changes effectively influence the economy to engage more in external trade or more in domestic trade.

These conditions were met much better at the beginning of the century than was to be the case later on. Firms seek outside finance either to facilitate the sale of goods or the production of goods. The former requirement can normally be met by short-term finance, such as trade bills of exchange, while the latter normally requires long-term money capital. Trade bills are as useful in the finance of overseas trade as of domestic trade.

Bank rate was the rate at which the Bank of England discounted first class bills of exchange. At a time when the bulk of the bill market consisted of trade bills, a change in Bank rate immediately affected trade. For instance, a rise in Bank rate meant a fall in the value of bills which in turn meant it had become more expensive to trade. Conversely, a fall in Bank rate made it cheaper to trade.

When production was competitive, and it widely was at the beginning of the century, firms sought outside finance for the sale of goods. A large number of small firms produced known goods which reached consumers via a large number of small retail outlets the world over. The link between producers and retailers was provided by merchants, whose task it was to collect goods from producers and hold the goods in stock until they could be distributed. Stocks were not held for long but were continuously replenished and depleted. Short-term finance was what was wanted to tide over the time gaps involved in such trade. Producers wanted to be paid when they parted with the goods or soon after. Retailers could not pay the

8

merchants until they were able to sell. So that the merchants could pay the producers and be themselves paid by retailers before the goods reached the consumers, bills of exchange were used. These are orders to pay at a specified date. If drawn on a reputable firm, there was no difficulty in encashing them at a bank or other financial institution at an appropriate rate of discount. Bill finance was then the finance of stockholding, and this was susceptible to the rate at which the bills could be discounted.

A rise in Bank rate set off a general rise in interest rates. A rise in the rate of discount meant that merchants got less money and producers got less money when they encashed such bills. In consequence there was a rise in the cost of stockholding and a rise in the cost of producing for stock. As the cost of stockholding went up, merchants could not afford to replenish their stocks at the same rate as before and/or at the same price per unit as before.

This forced producers to sell for less and/or to curtail output. Because there were so many of them, producers had to accept the competitive price prevailing in the market. Each of those producers could always make most money by producing as much as possible with whatever equipment he had. An expansion of output then meant that equipment was used to the limits of capacity. In consequence costs rose with each additional unit produced. In other words, production took place in conditions of diminishing returns. If producers could not sell as much as before, they had to produce less. They could do so at lower unit costs and so could sell cheaper. Thus, in diminishing returns activities, higher interest rates led to lower prices. It also led to less investment. Such firms' investment was financed out of profits. The last (or 'marginal') unit produced just covered costs, while each preceding unit made a profit. A smaller output at a lower price, reduced unit costs but also profits per unit. (A fall in Bank rate set off a chain reaction in the opposite direction.)

Through some sort of intellectual shorthand, it came to be widely believed that higher interest rates, by themselves, would always mean lower prices and that higher interest rates would always mean less production and, therefore, less employment. Low interest rates came to be thought of as inflationary but favourable to employment.

As often happens, conclusions which fit special circumstances came to be proclaimed as universal laws. Even at the beginning of the century, this picture did not fit every case. Nevertheless, it is a tolerably accurate overall sketch for a time in history when British industrialists directed their main energies at spreading their achievements through more and more production of the same kind of goods to more and more consumers at home and abroad. Short-term finance was of special importance and control of the economy by operating on short-term interest rates could be more powerful than it used to be in the more innovating period of the Industrial Revolution, or was to be in the new innovating age which followed the Second World War.[19]

It is not suggested that those engaged in traditional activities never needed any outside finance other than for selling. Often they had to go to their banks for finance of their day-to-day activities. There, accommodation could be obtained in the form of bank advances. These advances were a kind of carry-on finance rather than finance of new ventures so that, even if they were automatically renewed, they too were inherently a form of short-term finance. As such they were influenced by Bank rate. Throughout this century until September 1971 the rate on bank advances for private borrowers was Bank rate plus at least 1 per cent, on the assumption that Bank rate was never less than 4 per cent. Thus, any rise in Bank rate above

4 per cent restricted the day-to-day activities of firms. Although the rate on bank advances had a direct effect on current production, it also was a short-term rate and was determined by what happened to the rules governing the finance of trade.

This is not a full description of what happened in each trade but a rough outline of the situation in the major industrial activities of the time. The description also fits the finance of the import trades in primary products; until the late 1950s, three-quarters of total British imports.[20] World trade in primary product was centred on Britain, so that primary producers the world over were sensitive to British prices. This worked smoothly most of the time. Occasionally there were disturbances to prevailing values and trade. These disturbances took the form of sudden and unexpected upward movements in prices of primary products relative to prices of British manufactures. This raised costs and so endangered the prosperity of British manufacturing industry. It also endangered the balance of payments, since the rise in import prices weakened the balance of payments. Although the monetary system of the time fitted the requirements of the major import trades, there appears to be no evidence that the monetary authorities took any notice of the connection. The monetary and the trading situation fitted together so well that it was not worth talking or even thinking about. What worried the monetary authorities was that such disturbances might threaten the gold reserves. They altered Bank rate or took other measures of credit control solely with the view to maintaining the convertibility of sterling into gold. Perhaps this was monetary control for money's sake, but it so happened that the convertibility of sterling was at risk when the cost of imports was rising. At such times, the Bank of England could not be so sure that for every pound it paid out at least an equivalent amount would come in.

If Bank rate was then raised for purely monetary reasons, the effect still included an increase in the cost of stockholding of primary products. In consequence, British merchants would either not replenish their stocks at the former rate and/or would replenish them only at lower prices. In either case the cost of imports fell, the balance of payments improved and confidence in the currency was restored. This could lead to a rise in unemployment at home, but it also lowered the price of food. Hence the very unemployment a higher Bank rate created was also made more bearable as a result of higher Bank rate. Moreover, because it also lowered the price of imported raw materials, there were fewer bankruptcies in industry dependent on such materials than the increased cost of trading by itself might suggest.

Food and raw material imports came to Britain relatively cheaply because British capital had been invested in transport and public utilities overseas. This brought overseas supplies nearer to British consumers. Moreover, it made imported food and raw materials 'cheap' for the country since payment for imports included a payment to British investors, so the cost of imports was to some extent borne by means of internal transfer payments to British investors. An increase in Bank rate at home signalled that such imports would be cheaper or that trading in them would be more costly or both. British traders needed less money to pay for imports but more to hold them in stock. It follows that less sterling was needed for external payments and more was kept at home. This further strengthened the balance of payments. Moreover, the higher interest rates made home investment generally more attractive than foreign investment. Even if the funds that stayed at home went into government stock rather than to industry, the increased demand for government stock raised the price of such stock and so kept the rise in interest rates in check. This may not have compensated for the fall in industrial investment but mitigated it.[21]

The pre-1914 position has been dealt with at some length, because it shows the sort of conditions which must be satisfied if monetary control through Bank rate is to be fully effective. To repeat, these conditions are that outside finance is needed for trade rather than for production, that the chief means of such finance is the trade bill, and that overseas production and trade are also susceptible to London Bank rate. This is far removed from the present state of affairs. Although none of the points made here have become irrelevant, their importance has been overtaken by other developments.

Import and export trades still depend on credit, but often on different kinds of credit. The cost of stockholding may still be a predominant consideration in primary product trades. In most of those trades, London is still the leading financier of such trade, but the lead is now less marked than earlier this century. Trade in primary products has continued to grow, but trade in manufactures has come to grow faster. Imports of manufactures, like all imports, depend on how much money is available in Britain. But the trade credit to finance such trade may or may not be provided in this country. In the case of primary products, it usually is. In the case of manufactures, the position varies. As a rough guide, it may be said that imports of the more traditional kinds of manufactures from less developed countries are financed largely from London, and this makes such trades directly susceptible to the London bill rate just as much as the import trade in primary products is susceptible to this rate. But the trade credit needed for the finance of imports of more complex manufactures from advanced countries is more likely to be provided in the exporting countries. In consequence, such imports are still susceptible to British credit control which determines the total volume of British spending, but they are not directly susceptible to the London bill rate.

This still leaves the bill rate with a large potential impact on much of imports, though with least direct impact on the most rapidly growing trades in complex manufactures. That impact is not automatic, but depends on whether those trades are financed by British trade bills. Before this point is considered with reference to the 1950s and 1960s, it seems useful to deal briefly with the domestic situation.

Here the changed nature of the chief borrowing requirements of British industry further enfeebled the possible impact of Bank rate. Industry's chief need for outside finance is no longer to finance the trade in its products but to finance production; and in innovating activities this is not just the carry-on finance provided by the banks but the finance for investment. This cannot come out of past profits in the same activity. It must be taken from the proceeds from other activities, be they from activities in the same firm or from other activities lent through the capital market. A major reason for industry becoming more dependent on outside finance for production is that the length of life of activities is shorter. Cotton grey cloth could be sold for generations. Black and white television sets have sold for less than one generation and are already on the way out. In some products, such as pharmaceuticals, the life of the product is even shorter. Many of these products never get into the diminishing returns stage. In their short market life, the larger the output the less is the capital cost per unit of output. They are produced under conditions of increasing returns.

If firms borrow to produce rather than to sell, the function of the rate of interest is altogether different from what it is when they borrow to sell. They need long-term capital more than bill finance. They must attract such long-term capital to themselves and this will tend to raise interest rates in times of full employment. Further, they must take the cost of long-term borrowing into account. This makes them more cost conscious and encourages factor saving. There is growth and less employment in existing activities. To this extent the higher interest rate works in the same direction as in the past. But it is a long-term rate rather than the bill rate, and it is conducive to growth in new activities while the higher bill rate is only conducive to less employment in known activities.

In the circumstances of today, the long-term rate of interest is more likely to respond to changes in the quantity of money than to changes in the bill rate. The latter could affect prices, production, employment and investment in the traditional manner as long as the finance of trade was industry's chief borrowing requirement, and then only because most activities were diminishing returns activities. Once outside merchanting is not needed (or not available), there is no such link between the bill rate, the cost of stockholding, and industrial activity. There can be dependence on outside merchanting when the goods are known goods. But new and science-based products cannot easily be sold through outside merchants. Selling must be done by specialist experts who are normally directors of the producing unit concerned. It does happen that firms join together in employing expert salesmen but these salesmen are more likely to be engaged in scientific parleys than in the financial responsibility of stockholding. Generally, the more complex the product and the task of selling it, the more integrated must it be in the producing unit. In consequence, the major link between industry and the bill rate is lacking.

There is still a link between industry and the short-term rate of interest through the rate on bank advances for carry-on finance. In so far as this affects the possible volume of output, any rise in that rate raises costs. This makes it more difficult to lower prices. There may still be adverse effects on production and employment, which may lead to a situation of rising prices and falling employment. To counter this risk there may be tax allowances on interest payments—but then the rate of interest is less effective as an instrument of control over activity. If so, it has lost much of its main function.

Thus it was not so much that Bank rate, once so powerful, had suddenly ceased to be effective where it had been effective before. What happened was that there was greater growth in activities which depend on longer term finance than in activities which depend on bill finance. Since Bank rate was the basic bill rate, its effect became more indirect and slow. This was more marked in home activities than in external trade.

For a long time, however, the impact of Bank rate on external trade was inoperative, because the trade bill had largely disappeared during the First World War and was not to be revived until the late 1950s. Treasury bills had become important as an instrument of First World War finance, and came to dominate the bill market for the following forty to fifty years. They have not yet disappeared from the scene and may never do so, but in the course of the 1960s, they became relegated to second place in the bill market. While Treasury bills were predominant, they were held not only by home banks and financial institutions, but also by overseas financial institutions, including overseas central banks. The overseas holders responded to changes in the London Bank rate but also to changes in the interest rates in their own countries and elsewhere. This made the response less certain than the pre-1914 response of British-held trade bills. Probably more important was that any capital flows which followed had no direct impact on the value of imports. If Bank rate rose, there was purely financial relief for the balance of payments and no effect on trade.

In the 1920s, this divorce of monetary control from the

control of trade may have been unavoidable, but it had unfortunate consequences. High interest rates encouraged overseas earnings of sterling to be held rather than used. This did not help the export trades. Moreover, because of the volatility of those funds, interest rates were kept high to make those funds stay where they were. This limited credit expansion at a time of domestic unemployment.

The situation might not have got so much out of hand had monetary policy worked on London-held trade bills instead of on overseas-held finance bills. It is doubtful however whether the restoration of a market in trade bills could have averted the major crises of the 1920s. Bank rate policy had most effectively safeguarded the balance of payments when payments difficulties were caused by unexpected and sudden increases in import prices. But the great economic crises of 1921 and 1929 came when import prices were falling relative to British prices. The abandonment of Bank rate in 1931 came at a time when it could not have worked in the same way as at the beginning of the century, even if it had still worked as an instrument of control of trade rather than as an instrument of control of short-term capital movements which had little to do with the basic trading situation.

When Bank rate was restored as an active instrument of policy in 1951, this very separation of monetary control from the real situation was considered a virtue. The physical war and post-war controls were abandoned. In their place, there was to be an appropriate combination of fiscal and monetary controls for internal and external balance, with emphasis on the fiscal controls for internal balance and on monetary controls for external balance.[22]

The idea had gained ground that control over the domestic economy and over the balance of payments were separate issues, and that each could be controlled effectively as long as different methods of control were used for each. The belief was that the domestic economy would respond quickly to fiscal measures, but fiscal measures would work only slowly on the external balance. Domestic consumption would respond quickly to changes in taxation, and domestic investment too would respond to tax favours or penalties.

Budgetary controls were not expected to influence the external balance with equal ease. Attempts were made to promote exports through restraint of home demand and this included attempts to switch home demand away from goods for which there seemed to be a promising overseas demand. One way of doing this was through the appropriate changes in indirect taxation. Since goods already on order or in the shops could no longer be diverted, such diversion could not be effective until after producers noticed a drop in re-orders. This took time. Moreover, such policies always assumed that the outside world would always want to buy anything the British did not want at home. Control of imports by budgetary means was not really practical. Import duties are seldom varied in the budget but are imposed in special tariff acts and modified by trade agreements. Hence budgetary policy was not thought suitable as a means for controlling external trade.

Bank rate was not wanted at home. It was still under suspicion. Rightly or wrongly, high Bank rate was thought to be associated with the high unemployment of the 1920s and it was somehow forgotten that low Bank rate and high unemployment had gone hand in hand in the 1930s. Whatever the reasons, there was to be no really effective interest rate policy at home. If it was needed for external reasons, it had to be made innocuous. The way out was tax allowances on interest payments. If income tax was high for internal reasons, say at $42\frac{1}{2}$ per cent, and Bank rate high for external reasons, say 8 per cent, which pre-1971 corresponded to market rates up to

10 per cent, the effective money rate of interest was not 10 per cent but 5¾ per cent.[23] This is only three-quarters of 1 per cent above the rate at which private borrowers could obtain funds even at the depth of the depression. Bank rate was then left to have its major impact on finance bills and so would influence short-term capital movements to the benefit of the balance of payments. The home economy could be left largely undisturbed by it. At least, so it was thought at one time in the 1950s.

In practice it did not quite work like this. In the 1950s the authorities did not usually take measures to halt domestic inflation unless the external balance or the exchange reserves weakened. Bank rate changes came at the same time or near the same time as budgetary changes. In addition, each package included at least some of a miscellany of non-budgetary controls, such as hire purchase deposit requirements and building licences. The home economy remained isolated from the external effects of Bank rate, and to this extent the intention of the policy makers of the early 1950s was fulfilled. But since the external effects were on short-term capital movements rather than on the trading situation, the policy could continue to be commended only for circumstances when the trading position was sound and nothing but short-term palliatives were needed for the balance of payments.

The mere fact that internal and external difficulties tended to come at the same time, suggests that the internal and external economy could not be effectively separated, even at a time when exchange control was tight. When the latter came to be relaxed later in the 1950s, there was even less prospect of separating internal and external problems. A change in emphasis of policy came in the late 1950s. The Chancellor declared that 'the value of the pound at home and the value of the pound abroad is, in the last resort, the same thing and one cannot tamper with the one without affecting the other'.[24] This led the authorities to interest themselves more in money supply. In the absence of an effective interest rate policy this had to take the form of control of bank advances.

Nevertheless, even in the 1960s the authorities continued to react to balance of payments problems with Bank rate policy as well as with the usual package of fiscal and direct controls which were intended to contain domestic inflation or switch domestic expenditure. Although tax allowances still made Bank rate innocuous at home, the revival of trade bills from the late 1950s onwards, at least gave Bank rate a chance to affect the external trading situation. In the event, the effects of Bank rate on import prices were not what might have been hoped. Tax allowances continued, and the revival of the trade bills took some time to become effective. The sort of trades which are most susceptible to changes in the cost of stockholding were amongst the slowest growing imports. Primary product trades were less London-centred and subject to control schemes in exporting countries which made the response uncertain. But the greatest difficulty was in timing. For instance, from the autumn of 1962 onwards, import prices of temperate zone foodstuffs rose sharply, and it is now known that this was a major contributory cause of the 1964 balance of payments difficulties.[25] But not all primary product prices moved the same way and a rise in Bank rate, had there been one then, would have hit all alike.

Even if all import prices had moved the same way, so that the signal of coming difficulties would have been clearer, it is doubtful whether a timely adjustment in Bank rate was at all possible. Bank rate policy had evolved to lead the structure of interest rates but not to lead the trading situation. It tended to be used in response to disturbances in trade and not in anticipation of possible disturbances. It was corrective medicine and not preventive medicine. At the beginning of the century it performed this function with sufficient ease that the connection between monetary policy and trade was hardly thought of. Later on it failed to do so because it worked on finance bills only and left the trading situation uncorrected. As long as imports were mainly primary products, as was the case until the end of the 1950s, a Bank rate system working on trade bills might still have corrected the external trading situation, even if the domestic situation no longer fitted control through control of the bill rate. But, by the time the trade bill was restored, external trade too had become less susceptible to control by bill finance. The old style monetary controls no longer fitted the real situation, and new ones took time to evolve.

3 MONETARY CONTROLS IN THE 1960S

When the Chancellor of the Exchequer expressed his 'intent' to control money supply, in letters to the International Monetary Fund in November 1967 and May 1969[26], he reiterated what had been his and his predecessors' aim during the previous ten years. The earlier attempts had tried to regulate the extent and direction of bank lending, but had failed to get sterling sufficiently under control to restore its power of command and avert its fall in 1967. The intent thus assumed new urgency. As will be shown below, later policies were more ambitious in the aggregate coverage of money supply but abandoned the attempts at fine-tuning the monetary system towards specific purposes.

The new policies which were to be embodied in the Bank of England's paper on 'Competition and Credit Control' of May 1971 and, subject to minor modifications implemented in September of that year, took time to be worked out.[27] Immediately after devaluation there was nothing the authorities could do but to patch up the former policies as best as they could and gradually work towards a new system. The November 1968 measures discussed in section 1 of this chapter turned out to be the swan song of the former approach. Effective though they were, at least in relation to the balance of payments, they were too makeshift to be a framework for a lasting policy.

It seems best to start with a brief review of the sort of monetary controls at the authorities' disposal at the time of the 1967 devaluation. This will help to put the 1971 policy changes into perspective. Chapter 4 will summarise the 1971 policy and discuss the sort of monetary policy which might best fit the 1970s.

British post-war monetary policy can be divided into three phases. It was revived in 1951, revised towards the end of the 1950s and again in 1971. The revival was only a partial one. At the time, it was thought that the internal situation could be left to budgetary control which would take the place of rationing and other direct wartime controls, and that monetary policy would be needed chiefly as a corrective for the balance of payments and could eventually replace exchange control. Whatever the intention, internal and external problems tended to arise simultaneously, and the measures thought most useful for one or the other had to be taken simultaneously.[28] By the end of the decade, the authorities had come to see the internal and external problems of sterling as one problem.[29] References to money supply became more frequent at the end of the 1950s but there was no experience in working on aggregate money supply.

Inevitably, the first steps were tentative. Not least of the difficulties was where exactly to look for money supply[30] and the term itself seemed to drop out of the official vocabulary for the next few years. It was thought that what happened to bank advances was not only a major symptom but a major cause of changes in money supply. The bank advances which seemed most relevant for such policy were the advances of the London clearing and Scottish banks—henceforth to be referred to as clearing banks. These banks were concerned with more of the country's current business activities than were any other financial institutions. They were also most amenable to control. Since 1951 they had worked to the rule of keeping about three-tenths of their assets in liquid form,[31] being cash, call money and bills discounted. Any change in the proportion of liquid to total assets involved a corresponding change in their more profitable long-term assets, namely investments and advances. Monetary policy could work on any of those assets, but was almost invariably pursued with an eye to how this would affect advances.

For instance, one innovation of the 1960s was that the Bank of England would from time to time call for Special Deposits of some of the controlled banks' cash reserves with the Bank of England. The intention was to limit those banks' credit base (liquid assets) and so reduce the possible supply of advances. This should have raised interest rates chargeable on advances, and so reduced the demand for advances. A more direct approach through interest rates was a rise in Bank rate. This was followed by an appropriate increase in the rate of interest chargeable on bank advances and so was meant to discourage the demand for such advances.

Only if these and other monetary measures failed to produce the desired result, would the authorities impose quantitative ceilings on advances. In the event, they did, at first mainly through exhortations to contain the rise in advances, and later through orders to cut them back. The policy of the 1960s came to be known as a policy of ceilings. In fact the ceilings were an indication of the failure to secure the same results through interest rates. The authorities' main concern, even then, was control of what they saw as the most important component of money supply, namely bank advances.

This is not an exhaustive survey of how the authorities sought to control advances. It may suffice however to point to the limited scope of the policy. Control of the clearing banks' advances was control over only part of money supply. It left other lending institutions undisturbed. After 1961 there were some attempts at limiting their sterling lending but since this applied to a multitude of institutions with widely different credit structures, there remain legitimate doubts about whether they were effective. A cash deposit scheme similar to the Special Deposits was worked out in 1968 but never implemented.

The method of control thus discriminated against the clearing banks. Whatever else it did, it resulted in loss of business for the clearing banks to the advantage of other lending institutions. In self-defence, the clearing banks formed subsidiaries which could freely compete for deposits with other institutions, including their parent banks.

As far as the clearing banks' own business was concerned, there were several escapes from the rigours of control. For much of the 1960s the Exchequer was in deficit and issued Treasury bills to cover it. When the Exchequer was not in deficit, and at all times in the 1960s, the increasing supply of trade bills provided an alternative way of getting liquid assets. If all else failed, the banks could sell some of their investments, which consisted of Government and Government sponsored[32] stock rather than reduce their advances. They could always do so as long as the Bank of England was willing to repurchase any Government stock offered to it. One of the chief tasks of the Bank of England has always been the management of the National Debt. This tended to be interpreted as an obligation

9

to purchase when so much stock was on offer as to dislocate the market. Although this obligation was never meant to maintain the value of gilt-edged securities over the long period, it was thought to be an obligation to steady the market. It was not until 1968 that the Bank first ceased to steady the market, and allowed substantial short-term fluctuations in the prices of gilt-edged securities.

These loopholes would have sufficed to frustrate the authorities' intentions in relation to bank advances. They were not the only ones. Other loopholes included the banks' cartel and tax allowances at a time of inflation. Since 1955 there had been an agreement amongst the clearing banks not to compete on interest rates. They paid 2 per cent below Bank rate on deposit accounts and charged at least 1 per cent above Bank rate on advances with a minimum of 5 per cent. The first departures from the 1955 rules came in October 1969, when the banks raised their lending rates by ½ per cent even though there had been no change in Bank rate. What they charged was not a deterrent to most private borrowers. Tax allowances reduced the effective money rate of interest. Continuous inflation led to expectations that prices would never rise by less than 2 or 3 per cent a year, and often more, so that the real rate of interest was less than the already enfeebled money rate. This loophole was partly blocked when tax allowances were discontinued for interest payments to banks for most purposes, but it was reopened when the tax allowances were largely restored in 1972.

Since interest rates were no effective deterrent to applications for bank advances, and since it had also become known that from time to time it would be difficult to get an increase in existing overdraft facilities, it is not far-fetched to assume that advances were often arranged for larger sums than needed; and that, whenever there were expectations that new restraints were coming, holders of overdraft facilities drew on them to the limit, or at least nearer to the limit than they otherwise might have done. This made them old borrowers for larger sums. They could then tell their local bank manager that they wanted their overdraft renewed rather than increased. If at any one point of time, say, one-half of overdraft facilities are actually drawn upon, this proportion is likely to rise when new restraints are expected. The result is an evasion of the controls through anticipation of the controls. Moreover, while bank lending was kept cheap by the cartel and bank advances were often higher than needed, abuses became not uncommon. Old borrowers drew on those facilities and placed the money else-where, obtaining higher rates of interest.[33]

Altogether it would seem that old borrowers were not unduly inconvenienced until 1968 when exporters ceased to be exempt from whatever ceiling was fixed, but had to be given priority within the existing ceiling. The special treatment to exporters was given on the assumption that production for export can always be distinguished from other activities. A firm can produce evidence that accommodation is needed to fulfil a particular export order and get it just for that. If full accommodation is available for that order, the firm has much more ease in using its other funds for other purposes. Moreover, if the same machinery is used and the same people are engaged on production destined for export and for the home market, the borrower may recycle the borrowed funds without meaning to and without the slightest intention of defeating the authorities' objectives.

In the allocation of bank advances, some of the special favours to exporters ceased in 1968. Like shipbuilders, however, exporters had access to guarantees of their activities by special Government agencies, in their case the Export Credit Guarantee Department. Once such guarantee was obtained, the banks would give special accommodation at fixed rates of interest. These were not raised until 1970, when they rose from 5½ per cent to 7 per cent. Such credit counted as part of bank advances but is different, since bank advances are normally for the day-to-day finance of business and at current rates of interest. The burden on the banks was relieved through the Bank of England's willingness to discount short-term paper arising out of those special schemes, if the proportion of money tied up in such schemes exceeded a specified level of the banks' advances. Nevertheless, at the Government's instructions, the banks gave special favours in circumvention of the Government-imposed ceilings.

This is not the end to the list of evasions of monetary control through control of bank advances. It only refers to evasions by the banks (through selling of investments and their cartel in respect of interest charges), by the tax authorities (through allowances for interest payments), by the Bank of England and the Government (through special favours to exporters and shipbuilders), and by the public in its dealings with the banks (through excessive drawing on overdraft facilities and re-cycling of funds). At least equally important was that funds could be obtained from sources other than the clearing banks.

For instance, the general public could try hire-purchase finance, while business firms could seek accommodation from other institutions and through other methods of finance.

Of these, only the hire-purchase loophole was easily blocked. New hire-purchase regulations figured prominently in the various package measures which were applied to the economy in times of economic trouble. Such controls were relevant only to consumer durables which can be bought in this way, such as motor-cars. Even here there were no evasions only if the intentions were narrowly interpreted. Thus if higher deposit and interest rates reduced the volume of car purchases, there was nothing to stop the deprived consumers from consoling themselves with more gramophone records; and they could go on buying more records at the time when they would have saved to pay for the cars they could not get. There was diversion of demand, but it is doubtful whether this ever led to a reduction in aggregate demand. Control of hire-purchase terms was abolished in July 1971.

Nothing much was or could be done to stop borrowing from non-bank institutions and foreign banks. Although neither group was allowed to compete directly for the home banks' legitimate business in the home market, once accommodation was available for any purpose whatsoever, the total borrowing requirements from the home banks were reduced. Similarly, if large firms or large Local Authorities found access to the Euro-currency market (in which the British banks were involved), their borrowing requirements in sterling were correspondingly reduced and what they could get went further. The authorities tolerated this. After all it was not their task to reduce activity in Britain, though it could be their task to reduce activity which depended on an increase in the supply of sterling.

Last but not least, the need for bank advances was reduced at a time of the revival of the trade bill. This was actively encouraged by the authorities through a reduction in the stamp duty on those bills to a nominal amount. The revival of the trade bill enabled the authorities to reduce the supply of Treasury bills without inconvenience to the banking system which regarded bills as an essential part of their liquid assets. But it also gave firms an alternative way of financing stock-in-trade. Their chief need for bank advances is to finance the day-to-day business. This consists chiefly, though not exclusively, of financing stock-in-trade and the payment of wages. When bank advances were restricted and wages rose, the availability of trade bills enabled them to carry on at the normal rate. They now had an alternative way of paying for some of their day-to-day activities which had previously been paid for out of bank advances. This meant fewer shutdowns of firms but also one more evasion of control of bank advances.[34]

In sum, the policy of the 1960s was an attempt to control money supply. The hope was that this could be achieved through interest rates by working on the demand for and supply of bank advances. Because this attempted control through one section of the market only, it was widely evaded. In consequence, the policy needed the crutches of directives which were given in the form of ceilings, subject to special treatment for favoured activities. These ceilings were in effect, quantitative controls of one section of the market. It is perhaps equally legitimate to regard the policy of the 1960s as the first essay in control of money supply (because that was intended) or as the last attempt to date of control through interest rates (because that is how it worked). The policy was too limited in applicability and too riddled with loopholes to be effective. Gradually as the authorities were forced to block first this loophole then that, they began to edge towards a more comprehensive system of control. This led to the monetary reform of 1971.

Chapter Four TOWARDS
A REVALUATION
OF STERLING

I THE MONETARY REFORM OF 1971

The 1971 policies attempt to work through monetary aggregates and to let interest rates find their own level in the market.[1] By that time, it was realised that such an approach could be effective only if money supply was defined more widely than just bank advances, and if control was more comprehensive than just control of the clearing banks. Historically, the re-definition of money supply came first. The concept of domestic credit expansion made its official appearance in 1969,[2] while money stock came to be officially calculated in three different ways from September 1970 onwards.[3] Only when the new target of policy had been thought out, could new controls be introduced. Nevertheless, the 1971 methods of controls will be dealt with first, partly for the sake of comparison with the controls of the 1960s which have just been dealt with, and partly because it may be easier to see what the 1971 controls are intended to achieve once it is known what they are.

The essence of the 1971 controls is uniformity of application to all banks. This requires a uniform assets structure. The liquid assets ratio of the clearing banks was abandoned. In its place came a requirement that all banks operating in the country should hold at least $12\frac{1}{2}$ per cent of their assets in eligible reserve assets. Finance houses came under a similar rule which required them to hold 10 per cent of their assets in eligible reserve assets.[4]

Eligible reserve assets are short-term assets which the Bank of England is willing to turn into cash.[5] More precisely, they are assets eligible for conversion into cash by the Bank of England. This excludes cash which is already in the banks' tills and is no longer eligible to be 'turned into cash' and also excludes Special Deposits which are cash the authorities have deliberately withdrawn from circulation. Included under eligible reserve assets are: cash balances with the Bank of England other than Special Deposits, money at call with the London money market, Treasury bills, local authority bills eligible for rediscount with the Bank of England, trade bills up to 2 per cent of total eligible reserve assets, and Government securities with one year or less to maturity. Compared with the liquid assets of the past, notable omissions are cash in tills, refinanceable short-term paper arising from fixed-rate finance for export and shipbuilding and the bulk of trade bills. A notable inclusion is Government securities nearing maturity. In short, what is included is short-term Government debt and the purely financial call money. What is excluded is finance for current commercial activities, with the minor exception of a small portion of trade bills. If the purpose of monetary control is to influence the volume of lending for commercial activities, and the authorities do not wish to discriminate between various forms of activity, commercial paper has no place amongst the reserve assets.

Initially, the banks were well endowed with eligible reserve assets. The first bank balance sheets, under the new rules, were published in October 1971. They showed them to be at close on 16 per cent of total assets,[6] so that there followed some months when bank managers were unusually friendly to all comers. Finance houses, however, had none or next to none. They were given twelve months to accumulate such assets, and this affected especially those who had applied for recognition as banks. Their operations were accordingly somewhat limited during the transition period, but since some of them had experienced marked expansion of business after the abolition of hire-purchase control earlier in the summer of 1971, the effects may not have been unduly restrictive. It was not until mid-1972, that the banks' eligible reserve assets ratio came down close to the required minimum, and that of the finance houses came close up to it. The new policy could not be put to the test until then.

The test is how effectively the new methods of credit control work to expand or restrict total credit in accordance with the authorities' aggregate target. The means of control are Special Deposits and open market operations. Since Special Deposits were to be applied uniformly, all outstanding ones were repaid at the time of the inception of the scheme. Inevitably this meant that some credit expansion had to take place before there could be a call for Special Deposits and the policy could start to operate in either direction. It was intended to use Special Deposits more freely than in the past. A call for Special Deposits will force the banks and finance houses to have some of their eligible reserve assets converted into cash, while repayment would enable them to acquire more.

Open market operations are to have similar effects, but raise more complex problems. In the past, their effectiveness was handicapped by the Bank's 'repurchase obligation' which, as shown before, had sometimes enabled banks to respond to a credit squeeze by selling gilt-edged securities to the Bank instead of cutting advances. This escape became more difficult when the Bank stayed out of the market for longer than usual in 1968. In May 1971 when the Bank published its proposals for 'Competition and Credit Control', it announced that it would henceforth cease 'to respond to requests to buy stock outright, except in the case of stocks with one year or less to run to maturity', but would continue to do so at its own discretion and initiative.[7]

It remains to be seen whether this will pave the way for more aggressive open market operations, or whether considerations of debt management will yet make the Bank steady the market.[8] On this will depend whether open market operations or Special Deposits will become the chief instrument of policy. The following considerations may help to put the prospects for a successful policy through open market operations into perspective.

In the past, when monetary policy was led by Bank rate, what happened to the value of gilt-edged securities was the final outcome. If the result was too strong or too weak, the Bank would step in to correct the position through open market operations. In times of inflation, the result was usually too weak, so that the Bank would purchase any such securities offered in order to steady the market. With this 'repurchase obligation' gone, a more independent policy can be pursued, provided the market for gilts (gilt-edged Government stock) remains strong.

The market in gilts has the peculiarity that it is a market in long-term securities, some of them even undated, which are wanted for short-term purposes. The main motive for holding gilts is to get cash at a specified time. They are held by banks, insurance companies, and other financial institutions at home or abroad, by business houses, educational establishments and a multitude of other institutions, as well as by private individuals who have to meet financial obligations at some time in the near future. In times of inflation and rising interest rates, when the capital value of fixed interest bearing stock falls, there is seldom a case for holding them for long periods. As a rule, they are held because they are always encashable, and as long as the interest earned exceeds any likely capital loss, they are attractive to have so that the cash is there when salaries have to be paid or insurance claims must be met. This ensures a large and steady turnover.

A short-term market in long-term securities satisfies two requirements. Because it is a short-term market, there is a rapid turnover. Short-term markets are also sensitive to expectations. For both reasons, it is a useful end of the market to operate in. Because it is a market in long-term securities, variations in the supply of such securities affect the basic long-term rate of interest inversely. This effect on the long-term rate of interest affects the whole interest structure, including short-term rates of interest, until finally the Bank's lending rate must follow. What happens to the Bank's lending rate is then the final outcome.

This was formally recognised in October 1972 when the traditional Thursday morning announcement of Bank rate was discontinued. In its place came a minimum lending rate at which the Bank will assist the money market in its capacity as lender of the last resort. It is made known on Friday afternoons and equals the average discount rate on Treasury bills during the week just ending, plus $\frac{1}{2}$ per cent and rounded up to the nearest $\frac{1}{4}$ per cent. Effectively, this means that the Bank's terms next week follow the market conditions of this week. The new rate follows and does not lead, so that the position is the reverse of what it was when Bank rate led the structure of interest rates. The authorities have, however, retained the right to fix the minimum lending rate at a different level, should there be need for a corrective of the final outcome. Open market operations, once the corrective of the final outcome of Bank rate policy, are now in the lead.

The basic condition for successful open market operations is the strong short-term market in long-term securities. Variations in their supply then lead to inverse effects on the long-term rate of interest. If the strength of the market can be maintained when the authorities support only securities approaching maturity, open market operations will be the pivot of the new system of control. The inclusion of gilts nearing maturity under eligible reserve assets indicates that this is what the authorities thought they could do. Given a substantial volume of maturities in any one year, the intention may be fulfilled. In years when there are fewer maturities, the eligibility may have to extend to securities with more than one year to run to maturity. According to the expected flow and value of maturities, such extension is more likely to be needed in 1974 and 1975 than in 1973 or 1976.[9] Should open market operations disappoint, Special Deposits will be an alternative.

To sum up the new policy so far: the general target of policy will be uniform eligible reserve assets. The special target, within those eligible reserve assets, is intended to be long-dated Government securities nearing maturity. If working on the special target should suffice, there will be a simultaneous effect on the total supply of possible lending as well as an immediate effect on the long-term rate of interest through the relationship between the rate of interest on the various stocks—which does not exclude the possibility of a widening of interest rate differentials between stocks with different maturity dates, nor a widening of interest rate differentials throughout the market. Bank rate correctives may or may not be needed. Special Deposits also affect the total supply of possible lending, but with less immediate effects on specific interest rates and less risk of distortions of the interest rate structure. In either case, there is control over the aggregate possible volume of lending. Details within that total are left to be determined by interest rates.

Once it was decided to let interest rates determine what sort of lending there is to be within a given total, all special arrangements had to go. The clearing banks abandoned their 'cartel' and became free to compete amongst themselves and with other banks for deposits.

Thus the basic lending rate on advances ceased to be tied to Bank rate or its successor, the minimum lending rate. Instead, each bank can fix its own 'base rate'. There was a short time during the first half in 1972, when private borrowers could obtain bank advances at interest rates below Bank rate. The favourites of the immediate past, namely exporters and ship-builders, can still get fixed interest accommodation but, since short-term paper arising from such transactions no longer counts as a reserve asset, such special favours seem to be on the way out.[10] The black sheep of the immediate past, namely hire-purchase finance houses, no longer suffer special disabilities through control of the terms at which they lend, but are treated as ordinary finance houses. Last, not least, the quantitative ceilings are gone. No longer are the monetary authorities concerned with who is to lend what to whom, but only with how much is to be lent.

The 'how much', or more precisely the 'how much more' or 'how much less' is to be indicated by aggregate movements in money supply. Once more this raises the question of what money supply is. It will be recalled that the policy of the 1960s was evolved with a view to control of money supply, but all that emerged was control of clearing bank advances. By 1971, the authorities were better equipped with information of what money supply might mean. Two concepts had emerged. One is the money stock, which itself was calculated in three different ways, and the other domestic credit expansion which adjusted movements in money stock by what happened to the balance of payments.

The narrowest definition of money stock has become known as M_1. This is money which can be used immediately for current payments. It includes notes and coins in circulation and sterling current account deposits with banks in Britain (excluding transit items).

Wider definitions include near-money which consists of accounts which can be used for current payments with almost as much ease as any M_1. The chief example is deposit accounts which can be turned into cash at seven days' notice—and usually there are no difficulties in getting an overdraft on current account for a few days until money can be transferred from one account to the other. Thus M_2 included deposit accounts with clearing banks and accounts with discount houses, but this ceased to be a useful measure when the monetary reform did away with the distinction between clearing banks and other banks. The wider measure now in use is M_3 which includes all sterling deposit accounts, accounts with banks in Britain denominated in currencies other than sterling, private accounts with discount houses, British public sector deposits with banks, and overseas-held sterling accounts with banks in Britain. This effectively means all bank money and is by no means a new concept.[11]

As a measure of current spending power, M_1 is too narrow and M_3 is too wide. M_3 is too wide because overseas holdings of sterling are not necessarily intended for spending in Britain; deposits denominated in foreign currency can be converted into sterling at any time but are more likely to be held for spending elsewhere; while the inclusion of public sector accounts means the inclusion of accounts, which can be varied by the issue or withdrawal of Treasury bills and other public debt and so directly influence the total amount of money or near-money available to the public. Nevertheless, M_3 is the best possible indicator of potential spending power which has so far been worked out.

It should be noted that neither M_1 nor M_3 take any account of possible variations in velocity of circulation, namely the number of times any particular money unit changes hands. This would have to be taken into account in any estimate of the effective supply of money. The estimates relate only to the stock of money on a given date each month. A comparison of the results for successive months or years can serve as a guide to policy because it indicates changes in the *potential* supply of money but not the actual supply. Perhaps this is not so much of a weakness as is sometimes suggested. In general, values change because of changes in the relationship between effective demand and potential supply rather than actual supply.[12] The value of money is no exception. As long as it is known that the supply of money can always be adjusted to changes in effective demand for money, the value of money cannot rise. As long as monetary control was led by interest rates, it was control of demand for money with supply adjusting itself, almost automatically. Under such a system of control it is virtually impossible for the value of the money unit to rise. It remains to be seen whether the new policy can alter this state of affairs.

Thus, if it is desired to maintain, let alone raise the value of the money unit, one of the most important guidelines is to see what is happening to potential supply of money. Once this is known, the effective demand for money can be influenced through variations in the price of money (the rate of interest) which, in turn, depends on how much the public is prepared to pay for borrowing from the limited amount available from the banks. In other words, the new policy is to control the potential supply of money and to let effective demand for money adjust itself to that supply. This makes it possible for the value of money to rise—but only possible, not certain.

If the chief problem is inflation, M_3 is as good a guide to policy as has so far been worked out. It also has effects on the external value of sterling, since exchange markets too respond to changes in the potential supply of sterling available for conversion into other currencies, and not just the supply currently available. But not all sterling is available for conversion into foreign currencies, for the simple reason that the bulk of expenditure is on domestic goods. Although M_3 can be used as a guide to what may happen in foreign exchange markets (having due regard to events in other countries), for an explanation of what has happened it may be useful to divide M_3 into its domestic and external components. These are domestic credit expansion and the balance of payments.

M_3 minus the balance of payments equals domestic credit expansion. If the balance of payments is in surplus, that surplus is deducted from M_3. For a surplus means that fewer goods and services are in the home economy than have been paid for. Although, at first sight, such a surplus may seem to be inflationary, the difference is added to the exchange reserves or to the holding of overseas assets. In either case, this raises potential supplies from abroad at a future date. Any initial inflationary effects at home are at least offset by increased purchasing power over foreign supplies. There is no danger to the exchange value of sterling. In consequence, there is no external reason for interference with domestic credit expansion and, since today's credit expansion provides tomorrow's employment, domestic employment too is not at risk for external reasons.

If the balance of payments is in deficit, the converse happens, though the effects may be more complex. The balance of payments is still deducted from M_3, but since it is negative, an amount equivalent to the deficit is now *added* to M_3 to give domestic credit expansion. Domestic credit expansion has been excessive in relation to M_3. The excess demand overspills into the outside world and is financed through loss of exchange reserves or ownership of overseas assets. The home economy has less claim on outside resources and the outside world more over home resources. Unless the home economy can be easily adjusted to meet the new structure of demand as efficiently as the old, the worth of its output is less. The exchange rate is at risk and so is the present structure of employment. If less wanted goods continue to be produced, this endangers the continuity of total (home and overseas) demand, in which case unemployment is likely. If the authorities wish to contain such events and cut domestic credit, they risk unemployment.

Nothing is inevitable, if the appropriate countermeasures can be devised in time. To do this, the guidelines must be clear. Moreover, the guidelines can be followed only if they are guidelines to the chief problem of the day, and this may involve painful choices between the various problems requiring attention. As mentioned before, M_3 can be used as a guideline if the chief problem is inflation. If the chief problem is employment, domestic credit expansion may be a better one. Whether the chief problem is inflation or employment, the guidelines show the way to what is likely to happen, since an increase in bank credit is always likely to lead to higher prices and more employment in existing activities, while tighter credit is always likely to encourage factor saving. Matters are more complex when the chief problem is the exchange rate. The balance of payments only records what has happened, and the balance of payments in any one year is no indication of what the balance of payments will be like in the next year. It should be read in conjunction with M_3. This at any rate indicates whether the potential supply of sterling is likely to rise and this may help to show whether there is likely to be a greater overspill of British demand into overseas markets.

Even the balance of payments in conjunction with M_3 is not a perfect guide to what may happen to the exchange rate. One would have to look at other countries' balances of payments, their M_3, and would have to qualify this by estimates of other economies' responses to their M_3 and the different balance of payments effects. This must await further research.

2 TOWARDS REVALUATION

In the meantime, all that can be said is that revaluation starts at home. If it was not possible in the 1960s to separate the supply of sterling for home use and for international use, although the Government of the time was neither averse to tighter exchange control nor shy in introducing whatever measures of control they could think of, one wonders whether this will ever be possible short of complete withdrawal from international trade. If a country withdraws from international trade and wants home employment to remain as unchanged as possible, as all industrial countries did in the 1930s, there is a case for a monetary policy which lets the potential supply of sterling adjust itself to changes in the demand for money. In other words, credit can be allowed to respond to the rate of interest. This did not work in the 1960s, when world trade grew at an unprecedented rate and no country wanted to be left out. This called for continuous changes in employment, for greater efficiency and increased specialisation. None of those is encouraged by easy credit. A country which kept credit easy, impaired its efficiency. If other countries did not go equally far in keeping credit easy, this impaired the exchange rate. The monetary system had encouraged an old-fashioned structure of production, so that overall output was not of the sort for which world demand was rising most rapidly. This restrained exports, while the rise in money incomes encouraged imports. The exchange rate weakened. Had it not been for the weakening of the exchange rate, the authorities might never have intervened. As it was, they did so through attempts to restrain domestic credit through ceilings on clearing bank advances which were only one form of credit. Revaluation thus starts at home, and in spite of their growing pains the 1971 reforms may be the beginning of such a revaluation. By making the point of intervention M_3, the potential supply of money, and by leaving interest rates (and therefore the demand for money) to adjust themselves to M_3, the prospects for keeping sterling under control are at least much improved.

This holds irrespective of the experience during the first twelve months after the introduction of the monetary reform. This could only be introduced at a time when the banks' eligible reserve assets were comfortably above the new minimum requirement. There was a period when the controls of the 1960s variety were abandoned and the 1971 controls could not be used to tighten credit until the eligible reserve assets ratio had fallen towards the minimum. It so happened that, during the interval between the two varieties of control, unemployment was high and a sharp credit expansion suited the authorities on employment grounds. It also happened at and after the time when the dollar exchange rate of sterling had begun to rise in the late summer of 1971 and was officially raised in December of that year. By the end of June 1972 markets lost confidence in the authorities' ability to maintain $2·60. They saw M_3 rising and, although the balance of payments was in surplus, withdrew funds. What they ignored was that the rise in non-eligible reserve assets was moving the eligible reserve assets ratio towards the minimum, and that the withdrawal of funds reduced the non-eligible assets and so allowed the authorities to expand credit further. If this means that a way has been found to offset international capital movements, this should strengthen sterling as soon as the point is recognised. It may be noted that, when sterling was left to float on 23 June 1972, this was followed by a drop in the exchange rate from $2·60. But during the first four months of the float it stayed above the old $2·40 rate until October. If past experience with a floating pound is any guide, an initial drop should be followed by an upward movement. This is not a forecast, but only a reminder that both the external and the internal value of the currency will henceforth be gauged by movements in M₃, a point taken by markets in June and October 1972.

This does not mean to say that M₃ should ever be so tightly controlled as to stand still. There must be some allowance for the growth of the economy. During the years after devaluation and before the monetary reform, the authorities once kept M₃ too low. This was in 1969, when national income at current prices rose by 5 per cent and M₃ by only 3 per cent. In that year, the balance of payments went into surplus, and if the current account surplus is deducted from M₃, domestic credit expansion was nil.[18] Inevitably, this led to a rise in unemployment in existing activities, at a time when employment prospects in innovating activities were already adversely affected by devaluation. Subsequently, the authorities tried to rectify this by allowing for a more substantial domestic credit expansion. It rose to 6 per cent and 8 per cent respectively in 1970 and 1971. The 6 per cent rise in 1970 did not suffice to cure the unemployment problem, though the 8 per cent rise in 1971 seemed to be more helpful. It accelerated further during the first half of 1972. The increase in 1972 worried the exchange markets. Although the balance of payments stayed in surplus, it had weakened only a few years back, in 1968, when an 11 per cent increase in domestic credit expansion was inimical to balance of payments recovery. Thus, during the transition period from 1967 to 1971, a 6 per cent increase in domestic credit expansion was inadequate to maintain full employment and an 11 per cent increase was too much for the balance of payments. It does not follow that domestic credit expansion should always be allowed to increase by more than 6 per cent and less than 11 per cent a year. What happened during the transition period is probably no guide to what may happen at times when the monetary system is more firmly under control.

One point however may remain relevant. There is a range within which domestic credit expansion can be allowed without risk to either employment or the exchange rate. During the transition period it happened to be over 6 and under 11. Different figures may be relevant in future, but the mere fact that there can be such a range is encouraging if neither full employment nor the balance of payments is to be sacrificed.

The effectiveness of the new policy will, however, not only depend on the perfection of monetary techniques but also on the responsiveness of industry and trade. To this end, intervention at the long end of the market should lead to more immediate response from industry. And the response will differ from that expected in the past. When the chief need for outside finance was for the sale of goods already produced or in process of production, low interest rates helped. When the chief need is to attract money capital to industry so that goods can be produced, higher interest rates are more likely to succeed. Moreover, with long-term interest rates high, new investment is more likely to concentrate in areas where factor saving is possible.

At all times, a rise in interest rates militates against current factor use and in favour of factor saving. When there is widespread unemployment, this means more unemployment. When there is full employment, this is the only possible way towards further growth. Higher interest rates cannot force firms to reorganise. They may prefer to retrench. But as long as money incomes are rising, most firms are likely to take a rise in interest rates as a spur to reorganisation rather than retrenchment. Economic reorganisation means savings in the use of time, labour, and equipment (the latter being real capital). More often than not, this involves at least some new equipment to save the amount of factors used per unit of output. That dearer money makes time more precious, is really tautologous.

That it leads to labour saving is widely known and feared. That new equipment is also meant to save capital is perhaps not so easily seen, though a moment's reflection shows its importance: there is no point in adding to capital equipment unless output rises more than proportionately (or, in other words, output rises per unit of capital employed). Thus factor saving raises real income because more is got out of the economy. The rise in real income is the source of additional demand for the employment of more factors. The process can become self-sustained and cumulative, but the initial spur may have to be provided by a rise in interest rates.

In the present context, what matters is not so much how exactly factor saving is effected but that it can be initiated by higher interest rates. Since factor saving means more value created per unit of input, it is a revaluation. In consequence, any policy which encourages factor saving relative to factor use, is a policy of revaluation. This should start at home, rather than with the exchange rate. The events of 1971 and 1972 illustrate this: the exchange rate was raised in 1971, but this could not be sustained in 1972 because M_3 had not yet been brought under control. The example further shows that the sequence of events must be different when it comes to revaluation than in the case of devaluation. In the case of devaluation, the lowering of the exchange rate comes first so as to allow for the credit expansion needed for more factor use. When it comes to revaluation, the first step is control of M_3 so that interest rates rise and encourage factor saving. Only when M_3 is under control, is the time ripe for revaluation of the exchange rate. The exchange rate should follow domestic revaluation but should not be left to chance. In particular, it should not be allowed to drop appreciably which would lead towards domestic devaluation. M_3 would get further out of control and inflation be intensified.

To stress the point once more: a fall in the exchange rate leads to more factor use in relation to values created. It makes more work. Tighter control of M_3 than was possible in 1971-2 can lead to higher interest rates and, what is even more important, to factor saving. More value is created out of given resources. There is more intelligent work done. There is revaluation at home. The exchange rate can follow.

Interest rates should rise most where most factor saving is possible. In present circumstances, this is more likely to be the case in production of goods and services than in their sale. The argument turns again to the question of the right intervention point. The early twentieth-century British policy affected the cost of the sale of goods almost immediately and production more indirectly. The control of advances in the 1960s had its immediate impact on the day-to-day finance of business, which usually means after production has commenced and before sale. The channelling of long-term outside finance to industry was left to the Stock Exchange where, until 1959, new issues were controlled by the Capital Issues Committee, parallel with banking control but outside it; and later there was to be control only of timing which was exercised by the Bank of England. If the intervention point is the gilt-edged market, there is likely to be an appropriate response of the equity market in the Stock Exchange, but only after a time-lag;[14] and a further time-lag must be expected before this affects decisions to innovate or not to innovate. Even if direct intervention in the market in industrial securities were compatible with the new policy of monetary neutrality between various activities, there may continue to be longer time-lags between changes in monetary policy and their effects on activity than there were at the beginning of the century. Nonetheless the responses can become more immediate, the nearer the intervention point is to the end of the market which satisfies best the most urgent borrowing requirements of industry and trade.

If the impact on production cannot be immediate, the impact on values need not take so long. Once it is known that there will be more innovative activity or more sales, values adjust themselves in anticipation. Not the least important of those values is the value of the currency in terms of other currencies.

Again, the question revolves around the sort of activities which provide the exports and want the imports. During the first half of the century and until the end of the 1950s, Britain's external trade was largely an exchange of British manufactures for overseas primary products. The trades concerned did best when interest rates were low and selling was cheap. Exchange rate variations were contemplated with a view to selling prices. At the beginning of the century only interest rates were relevant, since all currencies were directly or indirectly linked to sterling. Later on, exchange rate changes could be contemplated, but some of the major trading partners kept their currencies tied to sterling, so that alterations in the exchange rate of sterling should not affect their trade with Britain. As their trade with other countries expanded, the ties weakened. Moreover, as sterling became prone to fall, adjustments in the sterling exchange rate could cause acute monetary embarrassment in countries which based their national currencies on sterling and so hastened the day when they sought monetary independence. Where sterling devaluation brought their exchange rates down they tended to respond with increased protection. As time went on, more and more of them started to export the sort of goods they used to import from Britain. The special links eroded. They were links through a trading currency, which was managed for the finance of trade. Once finance for production is the major consideration, such links are difficult to maintain without uniformity of domestic economic policies.

Towards the end of the 1950s, British external trade began to be increasingly an exchange of manufactures for other manufactures, and by the beginning of the 1970s manufactures dominated the import trade and not only the export trade as in the past. The chief trading partners became other industrial countries and trade flourished as long as it meant increasing specialisation between manufacturing industries and within manufacturing industries. Such trading partners do not adjust prices in their currencies because of anything that may have happened to the value of sterling. They buy and sell manufactures at prices related to the prices of the closest substitutes in each market, so that the volume of trade comes to depend on quality offered rather than on price charged (which is more or less given).

In such circumstances the monetary policy which helps the export performance is then not an exchange rate policy, but a policy which keeps interest rates sufficiently high to force factor saving and efficiency on producers of goods and services. In this respect, the efficiency function of the currency becomes the major consideration—although if this goes too far and the rise in efficiency comes at the expense of high employment, this will not be tolerated and the country is likely to withdraw from international trade.

In short, the exchange rate should never be considered in isolation from monetary policy in general. Studies which just consider the balance of payments often yield valuable results, but can provide only part of the answers which must be modified in the light of what happens to the total monetary situation and the responses of the various economic activities to monetary policy.

This does not mean to say that the exchange rate can be

ignored and be left to float freely. In each country, those engaged in economic activity work within a set of price relationships which are adjusted to the prevailing exchange rates. A sharp downward adjustment in the exchange rate sets in motion offsetting movements in factor and product prices, and until they have percolated through the system, the economy stands still. If rapid variations are allowed in either direction, the disturbances may be so great that the economy does not even stand still. Hence any float should be controlled and kept within limits.

On the limits of possible variations in the exchange rate depends the sort of trade which will be encouraged or discouraged. Where short-term finance is required to finance trade, the appropriate cover can always be obtained in the money market as long as the variations in the exchange rate are kept within limits. A controlled float is then perfectly compatible with a prosperous trade in goods that have already been produced or will be produced in identical ways, so that what is needed is short-term finance for selling the goods. In modern intra-industry specialisation, however, it can take a few years to negotiate a contract and some more years to produce a unique good. This is impeded by exchange risks which only the Government can cover (and then only if it has adequate exchange reserves). The degree of exchange rate variations then determines the nature of goods which can be profitably traded across the exchanges.

Decisions on how much to float or not to float are often politically motivated. For instance, when wider exchange rate variations were agreed under the International Monetary Fund system in December 1971, the European Economic Community countries decided to work within narrower bands from May 1972 onwards. In purely monetary terms, this can be regarded as a step towards the monetary union the European

Economic Community is seeking. Translated into trading terms, this means that intra-European trade is to be more of the science-based innovating type which needs finance for production, while extra-European trade is to be more of the traditional kind. As a step towards European economic union, this makes sense.

In relation to world economic integration it makes less sense. If the more valuable trade is to be more national (including European-national), there just will be less of it simply because there will be less intra-industry specialisation. Any country, or group of countries, must decide how much of that they want —and if they want as much as possible they must control the float within such narrow margins that it ceases to be a float. Once exchanges are fixed again, they can only be maintained by movements of real capital as well as of money capital. But real capital does not flow to a country which cannot control its currency.

In an expanding world, there is no escape from managing a currency so that it can fulfil its efficiency function as well as its employment function. Should the 1971 reforms succeed in bringing sterling more under control, it will become a more effective means of command and Government will be able to concern itself more with politics than with commerce. If so, money will not add so much to the frictions within society, economic growth will be less impeded and the balance of payments less of a worry. Even the *Oxford Dictionary* may be vindicated in reprinting that sterling is something of solid worth.

Notes

CHAPTER ONE

1 *Concise Oxford Dictionary*, date of first edition, see fifth edition, Oxford University Press, 1964.

2 Based on General Index of Retail Prices in December as shown in *Monthly Digest of Statistics*, January 1972, Table 171, Central Statistical Office.

3 London & Cambridge Economic Service: *The British Economy, Key Statistics, 1900–1970*, Times Publishing Company 1971, Table I, Average value index of consumers' expenditure.

4 Op. cit., loc. cit.

5 From $2·39 in December 1970 to $2·55 in December 1971. See *Bank of England Quarterly Bulletin*, June 1972, Statistical Annex, Table 27. (U.S. $ spot rate.)

6 Buying price £3. 17. 6, selling price £3. 17. 10½. For further details see e.g. R. F. Harrod: *Money*, Macmillan, London, 1969.

7 In detailed application this would involve discounting procedures.

8 *Key Statistics*, Tables A and I.

9 Lord Beveridge: *Full Employment in a Free Society*, Allen and Unwin, London, 1944, especially p. 46.

10 *Committee on Finance and Industry* (Macmillan Committee), Cmnd. 3897, June 1931.

11 F. V. Meyer, D. C. Corner and J. E. S. Parker: *Problems of a Mature Economy*, Macmillan, London, 1970, Parts I and III.

12 See Sir Ralph Hawtrey: *Incomes and Money*, Longmans, London, 1967; *The Balance of Payments and the Standard of Living*, Royal Institute of International Affairs, 1950; *Towards the Rescue of Sterling*, Longmans, London, 1954; *The Pound at Home and Abroad*, Longmans, London, 1961.

13 *Key Statistics*, Table O.

14 Op. cit., Table N.

15 Opa. cit., in 12.

16 *Key Statistics*, Tables L and N.

17 International Monetary Fund: *International Financial Statistics*; summary table on World Trade: value in Millions of U.S. Dollars.

18 For annual and quarterly balance of payments estimates see *Bank of England Quarterly Bulletins*, Statistical Annex.

19 There is a considerable amount of literature advocating more gradual exchange rate variations, see e.g. R. G. Hawtrey: *The Balance of Payments and the Standard of Living*, pp. 60–64 and J. Black: 'A proposal for the reform of exchange rates', *The Economic Journal*, June 1966.

20 *Key Statistics*, Table E.

21 Phraseology widely used by politicians at the time.

22 See D. E. Moggridge: *The Return to Gold, 1925*, Cambridge University Press, 1969. For notable exceptions see pp. 65–6.

23 It should be noted that the 'income school' did not really become vociferous until *after* 1925.

24 See e.g. the Chancellor's Budget Speech, 1972, *Hansard, 5s., H.C. DEBs*, Vol. 833, especially cols. 1347 and 1354.

25 Even Keynes wanted price stability.

26 *Committee on the Working of the Monetary System* (Radcliffe Report), Cmnd. 827, August 1959, para. 377, asserts this in relation to the cash base.

27 See op. cit. in 12.

28 Written with apologies to all plumbers, especially those who have given the author excellent service.

29 See note 13, and also R. G. Sayers: 'The Return to Gold' in L. S. Pressnell (ed.): *Studies in the Industrial Revolution*, University of London Press, 1970.

30 Opa. cit. in 19.

31 Op. cit. in 11, Chapter 24.

32 University of Exeter Agricultural Economics Unit.

CHAPTER TWO

1 For details see *Bank of England Quarterly Bulletins* and *Bank of England Statistical Abstract.*

2 The farmers were paid the difference between target prices and average realised market prices in the form of 'deficiency' payments. Market prices were largely influenced by import prices.

3 Protection was only being restored at the time and, in the case of food, largely in the form of quotas.

4 Except Pakistan.

5 Excluding beverages. Sources: *Department of Trade and Industry* and *United Nations Food and Agriculture Organisation.* For details of food price movements see e.g. J. S. Chard and F. V. Meyer: 'Fluctuations in Food Import Prices and the Balance of Payments', *The Bankers' Magazine*, June 1972.

6 W. Schlote: *British Overseas Trade from 1700 to the 1930s*, Basil Blackwell, Oxford, 1952, Appendix of Tables, Table 4, and *Department of Trade and Industry (Board of Trade).*

7 International Monetary Fund: *International Financial Statistics.* See also B. J. Cohen: *The Future of Sterling as an International Currency*, Macmillan, London, 1971, pp. 192–3.

8 For details see F. V. Meyer, D. C. Corner and J. E. S. Parker: op. cit., Chapter 26, section (4).

9 London & Cambridge Economic Service: *The British Economy, Key Statistics, 1900–1970*, Times Publishing Company 1971, Table E.

10 D. Gujarati: 'The Behaviour of Unemployment and Unfilled Vacancies', *The Economic Journal*, March 1972.

11 For a detailed analysis of factor earnings, see op. cit. 8, Part III.

12 Curiously enough this point has been widely overlooked in the controversy following the publication of P. Samuelson's 'International Trade and Factor Price Equalisation', *The Economic Journal*, June 1948.

13 W. A. Phillips: 'The Relation between Unemployment and the Rate of Change of Money Wages', *Economica*, November 1958.

14 Average weekly gross earnings per production worker in manufacturing establishments, as shown in U.S. Department of Commerce, *Survey of Current Business*.

15 Male labour (aged 21 or over) only, because the move towards equal pay at the time would exaggerate the rise in earnings. Source: *Department of Employment Gazette*; also shown in Central Statistical Office: *Monthly Digest of Statistics* (Table 164 of June 1972 issue).

16 If October 1967 = 100, then October 1971 for U.K. was 144·67 and for U.S. 123·48. Divide the former by the latter and multiply by 100 and the result is 117·2.

17 See R. G. Hawtrey: *The Pound at Home and Abroad*, Longmans, London, 1961, p. 124

18 Op. cit. in 8, p. 561.

19 For 1968 and 1969, see Central Statistical Office: *National Income and Expenditure* (Blue Book), 1970, Tables 1 and 19. Figures for 1970 corresponding to Table 19 of the 1970 Blue Book supplied on request by the Central Statistical Office.

20 Post-war as 19, and earlier Blue Books. For pre-war see E. H. Phelps Brown and P. E. Hart: 'The Share of Wages in National Income', *The Economic Journal*, June 1952.

21 Total wage and salary bills of manufacturing industry divided by number of wage earners and salary earners respectively. See *National Income Blue Book*, 1970, Table 18. Figures for 1970 and slightly revised figures for earlier years supplied by the *Central Statistical Office*.

22 See e.g. A. G. Hines: 'Trade Unions and Wage Inflation in the United Kingdom, 1893–1961', *The Review of Economic Studies*, October 1964.

23 On intra-industry specialisation see e.g. M. Panic and A. H. Rajan: 'Product changes in industrial countries' trade: 1955–1968', *National Economic Development Office*, Monograph 2, 1971.

24 Op. cit. in 8, Chapter 22.

25 In 1970, there were 5,830 thousand wage earners and 2,055 thousand salary earners employed in manufacturing industry. Source: *Central Statistical Office*.

26 Central Statistical Office: *United Kingdom Balance of Payments* (Pink Books). For 1947 and 1951 see 1968 Pink Book, p. 75.

27 See *Balance of Payments Pink Book*, 1971.

28 On the leads and lags see e.g. P. Einzig: *Foreign Exchange Crises*, Macmillan, London, 1968.

29 See e.g. *Bank of England Quarterly Bulletin*, December 1964, p. 256, and subsequent issues; and Midland Bank Review, *Annual Monetary Survey*, May 1965, p. 10.

30 See e.g. B. Hopkins and Associates: 'Aid and the Balance of Payments', *The Economic Journal*, March 1970.

31 *Balance of Payments Pink Books*.

32 Opa. cit.

33 The factual information in this and the following paragraphs is taken from the *Bank of England Annual Reports* and *Quarterly Bulletins* for the relevant years and from the *Bank of England Statistical Abstract*. Note especially the quarterly statistics of the balance of payments.

34 Opa. cit.

35 Ibid.

36 Ibid.

37 Ibid.

38 Volume of retail sales. *Department of Trade and Industry*. See Central Statistical Office: *Monthly Digest of Statistics*, January 1972, Table 112, and June 1972, Table 123.

39 See e.g. M. FG. Scott: *A Study of United Kingdom Imports*, Cambridge University Press, 1963, and op. cit. in 8, Chapter 24.

40 *Department of Trade and Industry* statistics of volumes of imports.

41 For details see Chapter 3.

42 Food, including beverages and tobacco. *Department of Trade and Industry*.

43 *Department of Trade and Industry*.

44 Derived from *International Financial Statistics* country tables. Excess over the year 1967. A comparison of British export prices and export prices of all industrial countries suggests an excess rise of 13 per cent in 1971. For method see note 16.

45 *National Institute Economic Review*, May 1972, Statistical Appendix, Table 19.

CHAPTER THREE

1 *Bank of England Statistical Abstract*, 1970, Table 19, seasonally adjusted.

2 The requirement to raise savings after devaluation of the currency of a fully employed economy has been demonstrated by J. Black: 'The Savings and Investment Approach to Devaluation', *The Economic Journal*, June 1959.

3 On expenditure switching, see H. G. Johnson: *International Trade and Economic Growth*, Allen and Unwin, London, 1958.

4 Gross domestic product based on expenditure data at constant (1963) sterling prices rose by 3 per cent from 1967 to 1968. See *National Income Blue Book, 1971*, Table 8. But, converted into dollars at £1 = \$2·80 for 1967 and £1 =

$2·40 for 1968, it fell by 12 per cent. Since it took about four years for prices to equilibrate the exchange rate, the true position for 1968 is between +3 and −12, and probably not far from 0.

5 R. E. Caves and Associates: *Britain's Economic Prospects*, Allen and Unwin, London, 1968, especially Chapter III by D. C. Smith.

6 Derived from *National Income Blue Books*.

7 Op. cit. in note 8 to Chapter 1, Chapter 19.

8 See e.g. Sir Alec Cairncross: *Britain's Economic Prospects Reconsidered*, Allen and Unwin, London, 1970, especially Chapter 4 by E. H. Phelps Brown.

9 Domestic credit expansion was approximately constant. See p. 148 above.

10 This is the argument in the numerous writings of Milton Friedman and his school, though there is controversy about the rate of increase.

11 The Kennedy Round under the General Agreement on Tariffs and Trade.

12 See op. cit. in note 10 to Chapter 1.

13 This is largely 1972 reasoning, aided by the wisdom of hindsight.

14 Advances and other accounts, excluding nationalised industries and items in transit, of London clearing banks and Scottish banks. See *Bank of England Statistical Abstract*, Tables 9(1) and 9(2).

15 See e.g. *Bank of England Quarterly Bulletin*, September 1969, p. 275.

16 For a first approach, see *National Institute Economic Review*, May 1972, Statistical Appendix, Table 15.

17 Bank chairmen were lectured by the Chancellor. The Bank of England 'fined' the clearing banks by withholding the rate of interest payable on Special Deposits.

18　For detailed historic surveys see R. G. Hawtrey: *A Century of Bank Rate*, Longmans, London, 1938, and A. Feavearyear: *The Pound Sterling*, 2nd edn., by E. V. Morgan, Clarendon Press, Oxford, 1963. For a brief summary, see Chapter 26 of op. cit. in note 11 to Chapter 1.

19　For an account of the different borrowing requirements of various British industries, see e.g. E. V. Morgan: *The Stock Exchange*, Elek Books, 1962, Chapter 8 and p. 203.

20　Including fuels. If these are excluded, primary products came to between two-thirds and four-fifths of total imports.

21　For a detailed account see Sir Alex Cairncross: *Home and Foreign Investment*, Cambridge University Press, 1963.

22　For the theory of internal and external balance, see R. Mundell: 'The Appropriate Use of Monetary and Fiscal Policy for Internal and External Balance', *International Monetary Fund Staff Papers*, March 1962. For details of British policy, see e.g. the *Midland Bank Review*'s Annual Monetary Surveys in each year's May issue.

23　I.e. $42\frac{1}{2}$ per cent of 10 per cent to be deducted from the 10 per cent.

24　*Hansard, 5s., H.C. DEBs*, Vol. 575, col. 46.

25　J. S. Chard & op. cit. in note 5 to Chapter 2.

26　Letters of Intent of November 1967 and May 1969.

27　*Bank of England Quarterly Bulletin*, June 1971 and December 1971. See also *Midland Bank Review*, November 1971: 'Banking Regulation and Competition—a Commentary on the New Arrangements'.

28　They were not always introduced on the same data. Some of the packages came in stages but invariably overlapped in time. Hence they worked simultaneously.

29　See e.g. op. cit. in 24.

30　These ideas only came to be clarified in the 1960s under the influence of the writings of Milton Friedman and the

Federal Reserve Bank of St Louis. For application to Britain see N. Kavanagh and A. A. Walters: 'Demand for Money in the U.K., 1877–1961', *Bulletin of the Oxford University Institute of Economics and Statistics*, May 1966, and C. A. E. Goodhart and A. D. Crockett: 'The Importance of Money', *Bank of England Quarterly*, June 1970, and opa. cit. there.

31 For the London clearing banks the rule was first 30 per cent which was later reduced to 28 per cent. Similar rules applied to the Scottish banks.

32 I.e. stock of nationalised industries.

33 *Midland Bank Review*, May 1970, p. 18.

34 The survey of evasions is largely based on the *Midland Bank Review*'s Annual Monetary Surveys and the *Bank of England Quarterly Bulletin*.

CHAPTER FOUR

1 For sources see note 27, Chapter 3.

2 Supplement to the *Bank of England Quarterly Bulletin*, September 1969.

3 *Bank of England Quarterly Bulletin*, September 1970: 'The Stock of Money'.

4 Different rules were applied to discount houses. See note 27, Chapter 3.

5 *Bank of England Quarterly Bulletin*, June 1971: 'Competition and Credit Control', para. 8, p. 100.

6 *Bank of England Quarterly Bulletin*, March and June 1972, Table 9.

7 Op. cit. in 5, para. 13, p. 101.

8 For details see: *Midland Bank Review*: 'The Gilt-edged Market and Credit Control: A new Policy but an Unchanged Dilemma', August 1971.

9 Op. cit., Table 1, p. 7.

10 Effectively the cost of the special interest rate was taken over by the Government in 1972, *Bank of England Quarterly Bulletin*, June 1972: 'The Finance of Medium and Long Term Export and Shipbuilding Credits'.

11 *Bank of England Quarterly Bulletin*, September 1970: 'The Stock of Money' and statistical annexe in subsequent issues. See also *Midland Bank Review*, November 1970: 'Another Look at Money Supply', and *Midland Bank Review*, February 1969: 'Money Supply and the Banks'.

12 This point has been made by W. A. Lewis in a different context in 'Economic Development with Unlimited Labour', *The Manchester School*, May 1954.

13 Derived from *Bank of England Quarterly Bulletin*, March 1972, and *National Income Blue Book*. Note: the balance of payments in here defined as the current account balance.

14 Gordon Pepper and Robert Thomas: *The Historical Importance of Money in the United Kingdom*, W. Greenwell and Co., London, 1972.

Index

Index

Printed in the United States
by Baker & Taylor Publisher Services

Printed in the United States
by Baker & Taylor Publisher Services